IN

THE PHILIPPINES

OTHER TRAVEL BOOKS BY MICHAEL PALIN

Around the World in 80 Days

Pole to Pole

Full Circle

Michael Palin's Hemingway Adventure

Sahara

Himalaya

New Europe

Brazil

North Korea Journal

Into Iraq

In Venezuela

In Nigeria

IN

THE PHILIPPINES

MICHAEL PALIN

HUTCHINSON
HEINEMANN

For Tom, Will and Rachel

A NOTE ON BAYBAYIN SCRIPT

THE PHOTOGRAPHS THAT FACE THE OPENING TEXT for each day's account have a textured background based on Baybayin, a Philippine script used to write Tagalog and several other languages. It was replaced by the Latin alphabet during the era of Spanish rule.

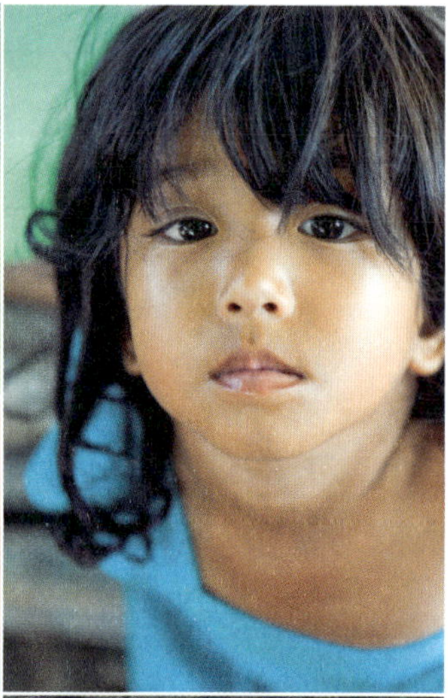
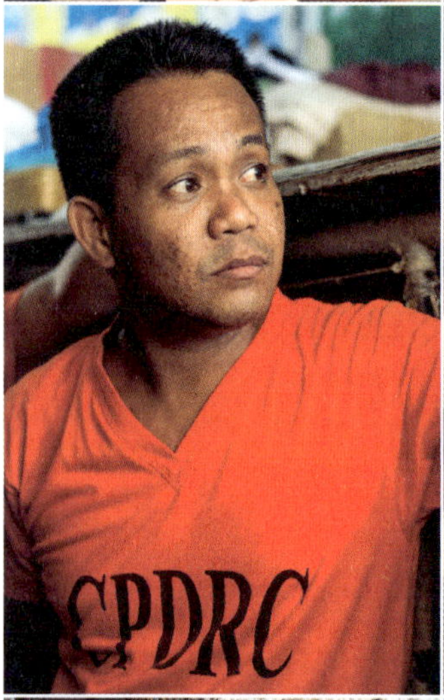
CPDRC
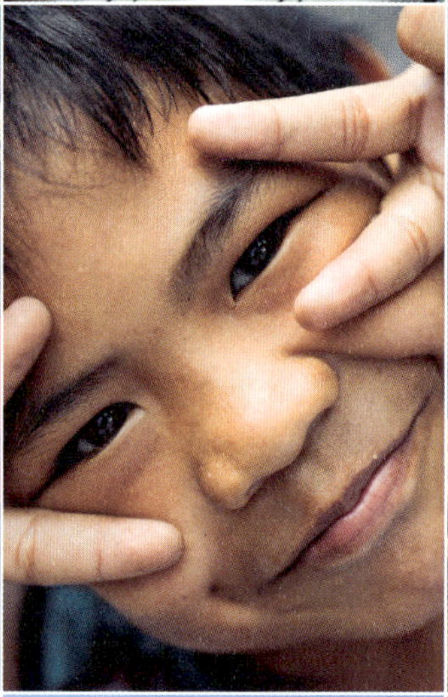

09

CONTENTS

INTRODUCTION

THE PHILIPPINES IS AN ARCHIPELAGO, WHICH IS loosely defined in my dictionary as 'a sea abounding in islands'. The four largest archipelagos, by number of islands, are found in Finland, Canada and Sweden, but the best-known and most densely populated lie along the 'Ring of Fire', a heavily active volcanic area on the margins of the Pacific Ocean.

Of these, Indonesia and Malaysia are the biggest, but the Philippines has over seven thousand islands – or as someone once suggested, emphasising their vulnerability, 'seven thousand at low tide, four thousand at high tide'.

The journeys I have undertaken in recent years – to North Korea, Iraq, Nigeria and Venezuela – have all been to countries largely defined by land borders. There is something very different about an archipelago. It's a land mass fractured, in this case, into seven thousand pieces.

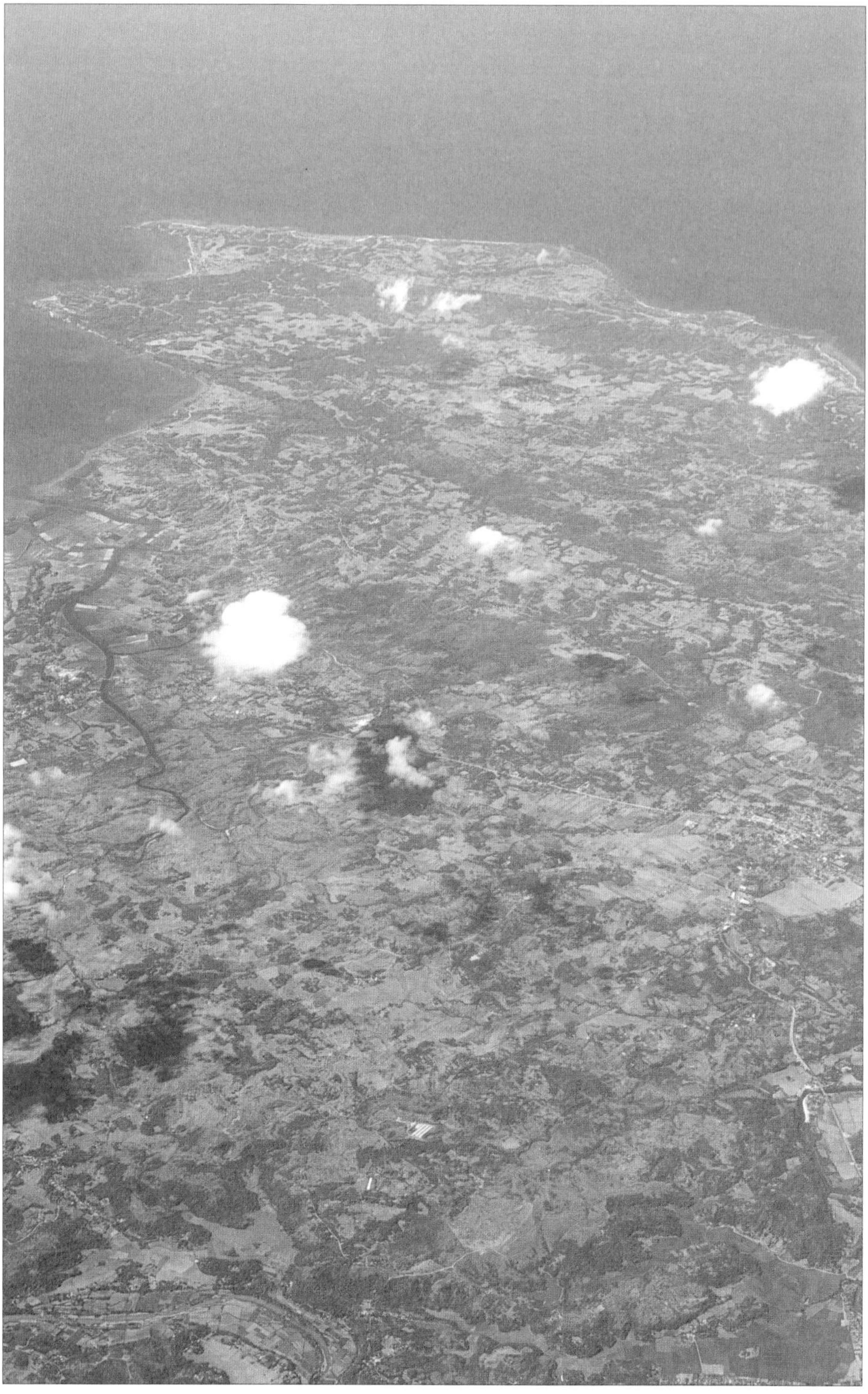

INTRODUCTION

As an islander myself I've always been aware of what it feels like to be surrounded by water, so when my director, Neil Ferguson, suggested the Philippines as our next 'country on the edge' I immediately felt a common identity with those islands far away.

Added to which, I had met many Filipinos working in this country and admired their work ethic and cheerfulness.

I previously visited the Philippines on my *Full Circle* series almost thirty years ago, but things have changed a lot in that part of the world between then and my return trip in 2026. Storms and typhoons have become more destructive. Regional geopolitics are now more vexed, not least the tensions between China and her Pacific neighbours over the future of Taiwan and the control of the busiest sea passages in the western Pacific. It was clear to me that there was much new ground to be covered. The fact that we would be travelling to the tropics in mid-February, and so escaping the gloomy chill of the British winter, clinched the matter.

And never once in our three weeks of travel did I feel we'd made the wrong decision.

PHILIPPINES
Philippine Sea
West Philippine Sea
LUZON
MANILA
POLILLO
CATANDUANES
LUBANG
MINDORO
BUSUANGA
MASBATE
SAMAR
Visayas Islands
Pag-asa (Thitu Island)
see inset map
El Nido
PANAY
LEYTE
CEBU
Mananga river
Talisay
Lapu Lapu
PALAWAN
Puerto Princesa
NEGROS
BOHOL
MACTAN ISLAND
Moalboal
Brooke's Point
Sulu Sea
Marawi
Pagadian
MINDANAO
TUGBOK
Zamboanga
Davao
BASILAN
Talipao
JOLO
TAWI-TAWI
Sulu archipelago
MALAYSIA
Celebes Sea

MANILA
CALOOCAN CITY
Smokey Mountain
QUEZON CITY
TONDO (SLUM AREA)
Rizal Park
Malacañang Park
Sheraton Manila Bay Hotel
Adriatico Street
Coconut Palace
Pasig river
Cultural Center of the Philippines (CCP)
Roxas Boulevard
Ninoy Aquino International Airport
Metro Manila Skyway (toll road)
LAS PIÑAS
0 1 2 3 mi
0 1 2 3 4 5 km

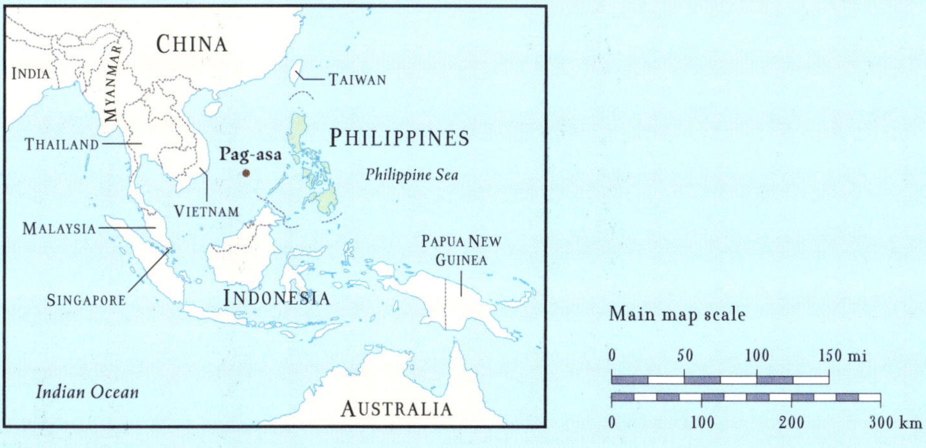
CHINA
INDIA
MYANMAR
TAIWAN
THAILAND
PHILIPPINES
Pag-asa
Philippine Sea
VIETNAM
MALAYSIA
PAPUA NEW GUINEA
SINGAPORE
INDONESIA
Indian Ocean
AUSTRALIA
Main map scale
0 50 100 150 mi
0 100 200 300 km

DAY 1

Arrival

IT'S A LONG, LONG TIME IN THE AIR FROM HEATHROW before the Philippines comes in sight. Over fourteen hours to Hong Kong, then just short of another two more to Manila, the Philippine capital.

Luzon, on which Manila is located, is the largest of the Philippine islands. The impression I immediately receive is of a solid and rather magnificent mass of jagged mountain ranges with thickly forested, steep-sided valleys.

These first glimpses are all-important. I find the whole business of flying, especially on intercontinental flights, more and more exhausting – an increasingly unwelcome reminder that I'm not getting any younger. But just as I think I should pack it in, I find myself, as now over Luzon, nose pressed to the window, looking down at a different world, with jungles instead of meadows, rivers plunging down mountains rather than meandering through gentle countryside, and sun-bleached beaches that seem to go on for ever. And suddenly the discomfort of being strapped in a seat for sixteen hours seems a small price to pay for being transported, in the widest sense, from one state of mind to another.

A glass of white wine helps.

As we descend into Manila the landscape changes and flattens out, and when we turn over the sea on our final approach, oil refineries, jetties, container terminals – all the paraphernalia of a serious trading nation – pass beneath us. Five minutes later we're bouncing onto the tarmac at the Ninoy Aquino International Airport, which if you go online you will find has been voted one of the world's worst.

Not just badly laid out, says one commentator, but largely responsible for keeping the country's tourist numbers way below those of nearby Vietnam or Thailand.

The airport's name, Ninoy Aquino, serves as a graphic reminder of the turbulent recent history of the Philippines. Aquino was an outspoken critic of Ferdinand Marcos, who first took control of the country in 1965, and who was once described by the media as funded by 'guns, goons and gold'. When Marcos declared martial law in 1972, Aquino was among those arrested and imprisoned; at one point he was even threatened with death by firing squad. He was eventually freed, but on the condition that he never return to his homeland. In August 1983 he ventured back from exile only to be assassinated on arrival at what was then called Manila International Airport. His political dynasty, however, survived in the person of his wife, Corazón ('Cory'), who assumed the presidency in 1986 when Marcos was voted out of office – and forced to flee the country – in the People Power Revolution of that year.

The fact that the name of an acerbic left-wing critic is enshrined in the name of the country's international airport says something about Filipino tolerance.

Unlike most modern airports Ninoy Aquino is not situated out in the countryside, but close to the heart of Manila. No doubt the cramped nature of its location explains why it has such an unenviable reputation for overcrowding and general unreliability. On the upside, the very fact that it is so near the heart of things means that once we have left the airport and driven just a couple of miles on the overhead Skyway toll road we find ourselves turning into the romantically

named Adriatico Street and driving up a ramp into the forecourt of the Sheraton Manila Bay, a tall, grand, modern hotel with a massage parlour opposite.

Later, to combat jet lag and get some sense of the rhythm of the city, I take a walk with Ryan, our security and medical officer, up Adriatico. I learn quickly that there are no rules of the road. In Manila the street is for everybody, with cars, motorbikes and delivery trucks sharing space with pushchairs, bicycles and Viagra sellers. Pavements begin and end quite arbitrarily, so that pedestrians – who seem impressively unfazed – have endlessly to hop from pavement to street and back again. As for crossings, these seem to be regarded by motorists as little more than a form of graffiti, rather than anything to do with pedestrians' rights. At intersections the priorities are vague, cars become dodgems, and fortune favours the brave. It sounds like chaos, and to a newly arrived Englishman it looks like chaos, but after a while I find that the lack of regulation has created a finely judged alternative order, based less on rules, barriers and flashing lights than on human instinct.

Infrastructure here is, at best, mercurial. The telephone lines, for example, don't run underground, but trail some twenty feet above our heads – an overgrowth of wires that run from post to post, bulging and sagging like tree roots (they're referred to locally as 'spaghetti'). There are shops of every kind and condition offering every possible service. And if you can't get what you want in a shop, you can almost certainly secure it from someone on the street. On one corner, a man in a Hezbollah T-shirt is riding his bike the wrong way up a one-way street.

What there isn't here is any sense of protest or confrontation. Situations that at home would be accompanied by noisy assertions of one's rights are on Adriatico Street simply accepted as being a natural part of what this city is, rather than what it should be.

BULLS

FUR BABIES ON BOARD
KEEP DISTANCE
BEWARE
I Brake For Animals
STUDENTS ON BOARD
PRIVATE
NWOW
PRAY BEFORE YOU RIDE
RIDE SAFE
Stay Humble

FRED
MARJUN
ISIDRO

DAY 2

Manila

THE MORNING NEWS CARRIES TWO BIG STORIES. ONE IS from The Hague in the Netherlands, where proceedings have begun against Rodrigo Duterte, the Philippine president from 2016 to 2022, who has been hauled before the International Criminal Court to face charges of ordering the extrajudicial killings of thousands of suspected drug dealers and users while he was in power. Despite his notoriety, he is still popular with many here, and his family remains a powerful political force. Bizarrely, his daughter Sara is currently the country's vice president.

The other story – which adds to the feeling of political burlesque – concerns the fact that today is the fortieth anniversary of the revolution that forced President Marcos and his wife, Imelda, out of

the country. The couple are reckoned to have milked the economy of billions of US dollars during his time in office, so it's scarcely surprising that on this significant anniversary there will be marches and rallies celebrating their removal. But there will also be protests against the current government. This happens to be led by none other than Ferdinand Marcos Junior, known to all as 'Bongbong', the son of the man who was overthrown forty years ago.

So where better to start trying to make sense of the country and its political dynasties than on an enormous rubbish tip.

For forty-five years Smokey Mountain was Manila's main rubbish dump. By 1995, when it was closed, parts of it were over 160 feet high. It has never been cleared. Indeed, it has now become such a permanent feature that people have built houses on top of it.

At first glance, it looks like a natural feature. Its sides are clad in lush green undergrowth. Small trees have seeded here. It could be a city park. But then you notice at its base the old television sets, car parts, wires, tyres, ripped-open plastic bags, shoes and discarded clothes that nature has not yet disguised. A local woman tells me that even though the mountain has been closed all these years, smoke still emanates from its depths.

If Smokey Mountain had stood in a nice middle-class area it would have been cleared years ago. But the labyrinthine slum – or, as the authorities prefer to call it, 'informal settlement' – of Tondo that sprawls around it is home to the poorest people in the city. So there the tip remains, while those who live cheek by jowl with it use it as a resource for all kinds of small businesses. Everything it contains that can be reused is duly pressed into service.

To be filming in such a downtrodden neighbourhood is quite a culture shock on our first day, particularly as this is an area where non-Filipinos are scarcely an everyday sight. Fortunately we have two brilliant local fixers, Girlie and Maki, to look after us and keep everything running smoothly. Their names intrigue me. Girlie could not be less like the Enid Blyton figure her name suggests. She is in her fifties, enormously experienced in film and television production and quietly authoritative with everyone. Maki is of a similar age. She has left her husband to look after her daughter back home while she looks after us.

We learn that the slum grew up as a first base for rural migrants from within the Philippines and, because it's near the port, for settlers from abroad, too. But over the past few decades, Tondo – and the Philippines in general – has witnessed a mass exodus, as some twelve million Filipinos have moved abroad to build new lives for themselves. In the process they have formed one of the largest diaspora communities in the world, responsible – thanks to the money that is sent home – for nearly 9 per cent of the country's GDP. Looking around Tondo, it's not hard to see why so many should have chosen to leave. The area is very run-down indeed. Much of the accommodation is down dark, narrow tunnels off which people live in tiny

WILLCHO
DUPLICATE
BY.MACHINE &
ACCPT.HOMESERVICE
09069518217

Open
ENTRANCE
WANTED BARBER

spaces. There is little in the way of welfare. Such contracts as are issued to build public housing projects are usually won by cronyism; their maintenance is left to those who live there.

But there's life and chat out on the street and a definite feeling of a community that looks after itself. At one stall an enterprising woman, named Doring, is selling recycled waste food, which they call *pagpag*. She tells me that late at night she and her friends trawl the big fast-food outlets like McDonald's and KFC and Jollibee for discarded food. Once they have brought it back home Doring expertly strips flesh from the leftover bones and washes it three times, before re-frying it with spices and ketchup and presenting it next morning on her stall.

She makes it look interesting and appetising, and if I didn't know where it came from I'd be very tempted to try a bowlful: I like a gastro-challenge and have eaten maggots and bull's testicles in my travelling life. But *pagpag* defeats me. I tell Doring, rather pathetically, that I've just had breakfast.

There aren't many facilities here in Tondo but, since it's the national sport, they do at least have an indoor basketball court, which sits beneath a high, threadbare roof. It's constantly in use, and when we visit we watch some skilful athletes playing fast and seriously. They play mostly barefoot – there are few smart trainers to show off. A little boy, who can't be more than five or six, is the lone spectator. He sprawls in a deckchair, but hauls himself to his feet when he sees us, asks me my name and then goes round the whole crew asking theirs.

After he's acknowledged us all, he smiles. 'I'm Daniel,' he says, with quiet satisfaction.

After lunch we cross town to Quezon City, another part of Metro Manila, and join dozens of police and press vehicles drawn up beside a road called EDSA (Epifanio de los Santos Avenue), where a march is being held to celebrate the protest on this same road forty years ago that resulted in Ferdinand and Imelda Marcos fleeing the country. Banners held aloft proclaim that this is the Fortieth EDSA People Power Revolution.

The Marcoses had been accused of corruption and misuse of government funds for their own private ends. At first they tried to tough it out. But when protests escalated and the state broadcaster was seized by demonstrators, they realised that the game was up. Offered refuge by the US government, they fled to Honolulu on 25 February 1986.

But not before they'd done quite a bit of packing. Two C-141 transport planes were required to take luggage that, according to the official 23-page-long US customs record, included: 23 wooden crates; 12 suitcases and various bags and chests that contained enough clothes to fill 67 racks; 413 pieces of jewellery, including 70 pairs of jewel-studded cufflinks; an ivory statue of the infant Jesus with a silver mantle and a diamond necklace; 24 gold bricks inscribed 'To my husband on our 24th anniversary'; and more than 27 million Philippine pesos in freshly printed notes. The total value was $15 million.

But the new government were soon to discover this was actually only a very small part of the Marcoses' wealth. In fact, according to some accounts, Marcos had syphoned off up to $10 billion while in office.

It's this huge number that is emblazoned on the banners of the protestors, driven, as they were forty years ago, by blazing indignation that a family so rich could bleed dry a country so poor. What is almost worse today is that despite all the work of various commissions set up in Cory Aquino's presidency hardly any of the money has been retrieved. The only – poor – consolation was the discovery of twelve hundred pairs of shoes left behind by Imelda when she fled. Rumour has it that she possessed as many as three thousand pairs, so she didn't exactly have to depart barefoot.

And to cap it all, the big spenders' son is running the country.

Most of the marchers look to be young, as do the police. Many of them were not yet born when Marcos was chased from power. There's a lot of noise and chanting and banner-waving, but there

seems little appetite for violence. Both sides appear mindful of the fact that the People Power Revolution being celebrated was also achieved peacefully.

But the sound of massed shouting still has an awesome power, and as the marchers come down the road and we race to keep up with them, none of us knows where or how this will end. We follow them down to a concrete-walled area below a network of interlocking flyovers where they are harangued by various speakers as the cars swish by overhead. Then the action switches back to where we first stood, higher up the hill. Here we come across a specially erected stage on which an older generation of protestors gather to sing the song that was the rallying cry of the revolution back in 1986. It calls for more honesty, less corruption and a new dawn for the Philippines. The man who wrote it forty years ago leads the singing, accompanied,

with loud and joyous reverence, by an audience whose social composition reflects that of the people onstage – what you might call decent people of the left.

Eventually, things come to a close and the performers leave the stage. All, I discover, speak English fluently – and one of them, Leah Navarro, a nationally respected singer who received the biggest ovation of the evening, kindly agrees to talk to us. She suggests that we go to a café run by her half-sister to talk over the significance of the day.

The café is the embodiment of shabby chic. The doors are of carefully designed pre-stained corrugated iron and the small space inside has bare walls and hard surfaces, as if trying to recreate the reality of the Tondo slums we saw this morning.

Leah, an imposing woman in her sixties, is a warm and articulate companion and clearly very much respected. I ask how she can reconcile the joyous celebration of the overthrow of Ferdinand and Imelda Marcos with the fact that their son is now president of her country.

Their son is not the same, she says. She grew up knowing the Marcos family and says that Bongbong is very different from his parents. They were obsessed with politics and power. He only ever wanted to become a rock star. He may not be the best leader they've ever had but he has restored democracy to the country, and for that she is thankful. She didn't vote for him in the elections, but despite her strong left-leaning opinions I have the feeling that she is happy enough with Bongbong for now. I tell her we've put in an interview request with his office. She wishes us well but looks sceptical. He is, after all, a very busy man.

As we drink our beer, I tell Leah how impressed I have been in my short time here by the warmth and kindness of the people I have met. Their default mode is a smile. And not a 'have-a-good-day' smile, but one that indicates a genuine predisposition to make some sort of contact.

She agrees but sounds a note of caution.

'We're people-pleasers, Michael,' she tells me. 'That's what we like to do. When you come here to visit, the welcome is sincere. The hospitality is sincere.' But she sees a downside. 'I think that works against us, too. Because we want to be liked so much, and we don't want to hurt anyone's feelings, there's a tendency for us to probably be walked over. And that's not the best thing for us. Sometimes we need to be angry. It happened then, forty years ago.'

A plate of food is brought over, consisting of delicately wrapped leaf parcels.

'These are *puso*. They're rice-cakes and crab in palm leaves.' It's a Cebu dish, she tells me, from the second-biggest metropolitan area in the Philippines. And it's good.

Then it's time to go. The crew pack up and head back to Adriatico Street. I ponder the crammed nature and the variety of our first day of filming. And I think about Leah and what she had to say about the country and its people. She clearly loves her homeland, despite its many problems. At the same time her willingness to talk makes me optimistic about the journey on which I have embarked. The Philippines, I am rapidly coming to realise, is not going to be one of those countries where it's hard to find out what people think. And that's very encouraging.

But will it be enough to send me into a post-jet-lag sleep tonight?

DAY 3

★ Manila ★

CENTRAL MANILA, THE CITY PROPER, HAS A MANAGE-able population of fewer than two million residents. The Greater Manila area contains nearly twenty-five million and is the eighth-biggest city in the world. And one of the slowest moving, as we experience on our way to Caloocan, one of the cities that go to make up the urban sprawl.

Once we have finally negotiated the maze of crowded alleys that dominates the last stage of our journey we arrive at our destination: a small house on two floors, with washing hanging from a narrow balcony. Emily Soriano, whose name is on the smooth-plastered wall beside a discreet doorway, greets us a little shyly. She's in her early

sixties, I imagine. Her son Angelito, we have been told, was shot and killed three days after Christmas in 2016 when police opened fire as they raided a house in which they believed drugs were being kept. She has said that she is willing to talk to us about what happened that day.

Emily is small. Probably no more than five foot. I can only marvel at how she's brought up a family in such a tough part of town. She shows me into her home. The red bike Angelito was riding on the night he died is prominently and permanently positioned on the balcony above the door. Inside it's dark and cramped and it takes my eyes a while to get used to the dimness. Once they have adjusted I notice that every nook and cranny of the confined space is full of things: illuminated Madonnas, a picture of the Last Supper, a goblin sitting on the loo. Then, suddenly, I become aware of three children sitting on the bottom of a bunk bed in a dark corner of the room. They are watching me solemnly. The presence of numerous toothbrushes by the sink tells me that there are others around.

Emily looks fragile, but I come to the conclusion that appearances may be deceptive. After all, she has managed to raise nine children, including her beloved Angelito. *And* she wears a 'Fashion Against Fascism and Fossil Fuels' T-shirt.

Angelito's death was not a tragic, isolated incident. It was one of thousands of lawless killings that took place while Rodrigo Duterte was president of the Philippines between 2016 and 2022. Determined to stamp down on the country's drugs problem, he resorted to a ruthless approach that involved heavy-handed policing and what became known as 'death squads' in a 'war on drugs' that was and remains highly controversial. Such is the Alice-in-Wonderland world of Philippine politics, though, that even as Duterte stands trial at The Hague his vice-president daughter Sara has this week announced that she will run for president in 2028.

Emily takes us round to the house where Angelito was killed. It's been sealed up, with the door crudely plastered over, and corrugated-iron panels stamped over broken walls. She fights back tears as she

relives the night when one of his friends rushed in with the news that police had broken into the house where he and a friend had been hanging out and had shot them both. He was fifteen and had wanted to join the army like his older brother. No one from the police ever got in touch with her, let alone apologised for the loss of her boy.

Curious locals pass by – young men and women of Angelito's age on their bicycles. This remains a poor part of town, and I can't help feeling that the children watching us are as vulnerable to anyone dealing drugs as they ever were.

Even so, there is hope. In 1985, nearly 50 per cent of the population lived in poverty. Now it's estimated the number has tumbled to 15 per cent. Current predictions suggest that that figure will continue to fall. Things do seem to be improving.

We say goodbye to Emily and climb back into our vehicles. The traffic is bad, and by the time we get back to the centre of Manila dusk is approaching. But we still have time to make a detour along Roxas Boulevard to take a look at the colossal buildings that Imelda Marcos had built in the 1970s and '80s as part of her bid to transform Manila into a world-class city. In the dying light, some appear as no more than massive shapes; others are floodlit. I learn that the Film Center, which she hoped would be the Cannes of the East, was built in a matter of months by a huge workforce, many of whom perished when a concrete roof that had not been given sufficient time to dry fell on top of them. It was nine hours before ambulances were allowed on site. Urban legend says most of the bodies were never recovered.

Even bigger than the Film Center was the CCP – the Cultural Center of the Philippines. Then there were two or three grand hotels, and the Coconut Palace that was built to accommodate VIPs – not least Pope John Paul II during his visit to the Philippines in 1973 (though he thought it too opulent and chose to stay elsewhere). All these and more lavishly expensive buildings, viewed by Imelda's many critics as evidence of her 'edifice complex', were financed by foreign loans that, by the time she and her husband went into exile, had reached a staggering $28.3 billion.

They were built for display, and doubtless Imelda, now in her nineties, would be glad that we made a special effort to visit them. Tondo, Smokey Mountain and Emily's cramped rooms in Caloocan are a side of Manila that she would not have wanted us to see.

DAY

4

★ **Manila** *to* **Palawan** ★

IT'S TIME TO TEAR OURSELVES AWAY FROM THE MAGNET of Manila and explore the riches of the archipelago, so we're at the airport early for a flight to somewhere that sounds as complete a contrast to urban life as one could find. El Nido is a town on the northern end of the long, thin island of Palawan, a UNESCO Biosphere Reserve that travellers to the Philippines almost unanimously describe as the perfect getaway. The name El Nido, which means 'the nest', refers to the edible swift's nests that abundantly dot the area's strikingly steep cliffs and that are in such demand in Chinese cuisine.

It transpires that this corner of the Philippines is seductively difficult to get to. Our aircraft, operated, appropriately enough, by AirSWIFT (part of Cebu Pacific), is a small twin-prop, and space onboard is so limited that our team has to be split between two flights, an hour apart. It transpires that I'm to be on the second flight.

Nearly ninety minutes after we have taken off, we're gliding in neatly enough over blue waters before cracking down hard on a short tarmac runway, all brakes blazing. At least we've landed on time. The plane carrying the rest of the crew had to circle for almost an hour before the crosswinds had subsided to the point where it was judged safe to land. All of which shows that we are very definitely no longer on the beaten track. But then that is the reason why we undertake these journeys.

El Nido is a small town that serves as a base for those tourists who want to get away from it all and explore the almost infinite number of little bays carved out of the island's spectacular rock stacks. We'll be doing something similar, but whereas the people milling around us have hotels to return to, we shall be going back to nature for a night in the company of Eddie Agamos.

Eddie founded a travel company called Tao Philippines to provide an alternative to mass tourism. He picks us up from a quiet beach, away from the crowded harbour. This sounds idyllic, but because beaches don't, of course, have jetties, we have to wade knee-deep into the sea and then, in my case, make a rather graceless scramble onto the boat in half-soaked jeans, cursing the fact that I failed to pack shorts. We travel, as most people do here when criss-crossing between islands, in traditional wooden boats called *bangkas*.

These use the catamaran principle of distributing the weight onto twin hulls, creating a shallow draught well suited to negotiating the region's sandy beaches.

We pass by sheer cliffs and pristine turquoise waters. All lie within the Biosphere Reserve and so are theoretically protected, but I can sense Eddie's frustration that developments have been allowed on certain bays, and that others have become popular beauty spots that attract a succession of visitors who briefly go ashore, take photos and then head back to town.

Eddie's philosophy is embodied in the camp he has created on Cadlao Island, which lies just a short distance across the sea from El Nido. Tucked in at the heart of a most beautiful bay, the accommodation is built of local materials, mainly straw thatch, palm leaves and

bamboo. There is no electricity or running water. As the sun goes down, we gather by candlelight round a long table and drink beers or gin and tonics, while a huge fish smoulders on an open fire. Great happiness.

In the growing twilight, I notice a mighty rock half a mile out to sea. It seems rather comforting, as though it's guarding the bay. But I then realise that what first attracted my glance was an oddly bright glow, partly shielded by the rock, way out on the water and still shining. I ask Eddie about it. He tells me that the light is most likely coming from one of the armada of Chinese trawlers and fishing protection vessels that move up and down the coast, staking their claim to the waters through which they pass.

I climb up bamboo steps into my attractive, though unlit, palm-thatched hut. I'm looking forward to sleeping to the sound of waves lapping on the beach. Unfortunately at my age the bladder never sleeps and I'm up and down the bamboo steps more than once during the night. The toilet (non-flushing) is a fair way off, and with no light – apart from my phone torch (which falls to the floor of the non-flushing toilet) – and a mosquito net to extricate myself from as I climb out of my hut, the whole operation proves very tricky. Returning from my third outing I slip on the steps and feel blood oozing from a cut on my shin. It's then I realise, all too painfully, that you really can't go from the Sheraton Manila Bay to an all-nature camp in one night. I find some Savlon and a piece of plaster to stem the bleeding.

I know just how bad things are when the sound of the gently lapping waves becomes a bloody nuisance.

DAY 5

★ Palawan ★

AT DAWN IT ALL SEEMS WORTH IT AGAIN. IT'S NOW 6.35 and I'm walking along the shore, coffee in hand, in the crab-like embrace of steep, jungle-clad mountains that curve behind me. The night was a bad dream. This morning, with the sun slowly rising over a placid sea, is a reminder why I still go travelling. Beneath the trees a Philippine breakfast is laid out for us. We eat off banana leaves and coconuts sliced in half so that we can drink their juice before using them as bowls for the various fruits of the forest we are offered.

But there are problems even in this little corner of paradise. 'Hell', as Jean-Paul Sartre once put it, 'is other people', and for Eddie, who has committed himself to design and build from and with nature, 'other people' are the developers who don't share his vision and who bend rules and grease palms to acquire land on which they can then build – to his mind, wholly inappropriate – properties. One such development, which lies in a previously forested area irritatingly close to his camp, consists of white-painted villas and beachside bungalows. It looks to be abandoned.

In theory, there are strict curbs on this sort of building within the Palawan Reserve but Eddie feels he's fighting a constant battle with those who ignore them.

Paradise lost, we load our gear onto two *bangkas* and head back to El Nido town to pick up vehicles for the next leg of what I feel is becoming an increasingly breathless journey.

Once in El Nido harbour we're back among the crowds. The ferry to Manila is at the dockside, a grey-hulled Philippine navy ship alongside it. Dozens of *bangkas* hover offshore, waiting for a gap to

squeeze through. Ryan, our medic, dresses my bloodied – though fortunately superficial – wound. But last night's toilet escapades have left me feeling very tired. Rarely have I looked forward so much to being able to doze in a vehicle for a few hours.

We're now heading to Puerto Princesa, Palawan's largest and busiest town. Our journey there takes us through countryside that is lush and tropical and rather beautiful. And Puerto Princesa, I'm informed, has some delights of its own, not least a four-mile

'Underground River', a UNESCO World Heritage Site that runs through caves and tunnels and contains an extraordinary gallery of natural sculptures.

I'm always a little sceptical about the almost fanatically enthusiastic claims made for 'nature' trails such as this, but from the moment our guide Raffy paddles me across a small and peaceful lagoon and enters a dark cleft in a towering wall of limestone I find it quite magical. We move slowly, taking care not to disturb the legions of

bats that twist and turn and skid above our heads. What the slow drip of water has done over millions of years is to create startling shapes and wondrous designs which, being the humans that we are, we want to try and interpret as something from our own world. For me colossal stalactites become massive stone chandeliers, stalagmites become tables and chairs. For Raffy, who lives in a country where 79 per cent of the population are Catholic, everything we see is a geological confirmation of his religion. As we enter a huge cave called the Cathedral, he points out a Madonna and child, an altar, a priest and, high on the cave wall, barely visible even with a torch, is Christ on the Cross.

But he's not puritanical. And he throws in a Hollywood reference for the tourists.

'Over there is a sexy woman. She's made of stone, so we call her Sharon.'

As we leave the silent beauty of the caves I find myself thinking that compared to all the wonderful sculptures carved by men and women throughout history, these extraordinary rock figures and designs shaped by millions of years of dripping water are on an altogether different and breathtaking level.

The caves are a comforting escape from the outside world and all its problems. But reality cannot be avoided for long. As we reach our hotel, word is coming in from the other side of the world that Iran's Ayatollah Ali Khamenei has been killed.

ANAK NG RANCHO
SEVILLA
ΥΦΣ
BOY
COMPANY
LHING

DAY 6

Palawan *to* Pag-asa

WE'RE UP EARLY – IT'S NOT YET 7 A.M. – AND AS THE GRIM news rolls in from the Middle East of rockets and air-strikes, we are, by strange coincidence, on the road to the Philippine air-force base in Puerto Princesa. After long negotiations we have been given permission to film on one of the tiniest but most important islands in the Philippines, Pag-asa. Only around a tenth of a square mile in area, and over three hundred miles away from Palawan, it lies in waters over which both the Philippines and China claim to exercise authority. At stake is control of a stretch of ocean through which passes around a quarter of world trade.

For the Chinese these waters are the South China Sea. For the Filipinos they're the West Philippine Sea.

With that dispute in my mind, alongside today's news from Iran, I can't help thinking that the world feels particularly febrile this morning. But as we pass through narrow lanes towards the base, my mood lightens a little. Roadside life goes on. A dog stretches its legs. Washing is being hung out. Bamboo shoots are being loaded onto a battered truck. The signs flash by: 'Washy-Washy Club', 'Pet Shop', 'Twin Body Massage'.

Eventually, and surprisingly, at the end of one of these Beatrix Potter-like lanes, lies the entrance to the HQ of the 570th Air Base Group of the Philippine Air Force.

I expect super-charged security and demands to see papers and passports, but one thing the Filipinos are not is officious. We are greeted warmly and shown into an area where food and supplies are being assembled that will accompany us on the flight to Pag-asa. We ourselves have to be largely self-sufficient, so we've brought boxes of essentials like beer for our own use. We will also be carrying some gifts for the people – all four hundred of them – who live on Pag-asa.

Then word comes that we will not be flying out on one of the big C-130 supply planes, but on a much smaller twin-prop nineteen-seater. Weight limits are tight. Sacrifices will have to be made. The beer is the first to go.

A weather update forecasts 39/40°C on the island, much hotter than here. Flying time will be close on two hours. Our aircraft is not quite ready. In fact, it's up in the air. We're told, rather alarmingly, that they're 'trying it out'.

Eventually, its flight worthiness approved, we walk out onto the tarmac and board up a ramp at the rear. We squeeze ourselves in as tight as possible, sitting in rows that, in military fashion, face each other. I can't help wondering whether I'm going to be invited to make a parachute jump.

After a nearly two-hour flight amid an eternity of noise and non-air conditioning, we begin our descent towards the speck in the ocean that is Pag-asa. The runway – a proper well-laid concrete strip, clearly built for the biggest and fastest planes – is longer than

the island itself. Once we've landed, we taxi to a hangar, the largest building on the island, and then disembark into scorching 40°C sunshine, from which there is little shade apart from the occasional palm tree. At the top of a thirty-foot pole an enormous Philippine flag flaps in a gentle breeze.

Pag-asa essentially comprises two strips, the airstrip and, running parallel to it, the human strip. The latter consists of various official buildings (including one that houses a school) and a big public

hall area called the Evacuation Centre – one of a number I've noticed while I've been in the Philippines and a reminder of just how vulnerable the country is to ferocious storms and devastating typhoons. Many of these buildings date back to the 1970s when people were first brought here to build an infrastructure around the base, and it has to be said that they are looking their age. They're now being replaced, and much of the island is therefore currently a building site. I've never been anywhere in the world quite like it.

Behind the strip of public buildings, and just a couple of hundred yards from where the most advanced fighter jets and the heaviest transport planes come and go, is Main Street Pag-asa. Here is where the nearly four hundred Pagasans who work on the island have built up a lively, genial, rural community. When we arrive a group of them is gathered in the shade of an all-embracing mangrove tree, while someone at the karaoke bar is boozily splitting the late-afternoon calm with one tragic Country and Western ballad after another. Side streets are lined with stalls, and families sit outside and gossip.

A five-minute walk takes me to the far side of the island, where there is a small stretch of beach and, further on, a walled harbour. It is from here that I can quite clearly make out a flotilla of Chinese ships a mile or so offshore. One stands out in particular: neither trawler nor passing freighter, her white-painted superstructure catches the light as she rides at anchor. She is undoubtedly watching us.

The authorities in Beijing continue to press their claim to 90 per cent of these waters, invoking what they call the Nine Dash Line, an arbitrary boundary that encompasses waters off the Philippines, Vietnam, Brunei and Malaysia. The Permanent Court of Arbitration may have rejected China's claims to these waters back in 2016 as having no legal basis, but the Chinese have taken no notice. What is

happening off Pag-asa is a confrontation between the rule of international law and the raw reality of power.

As I shift my gaze from the Chinese ships out at sea to the island's harbour, I spot a small grey coastguard ship at anchor which some children seem to have to themselves. They're having a wonderful time, climbing on board, chasing each other around the deck and diving into the water with great shouts.

They're not yet ready for guests on Pag-asa, and after we've eaten it's another night without much in the way of creature comforts as we all bunk up together on low beds and mattresses in temporary accommodation.

DAY 7

Pag-asa

DESPITE THE MOST BASIC OF FACILITIES I SLEPT AS well as I have on this trip so far. I have a morning wash with the help of one and a half plastic bottles of water saved up from the night before, then walk to the Evacuation Centre for breakfast. It's Monday morning, the start of the week, and at seven o'clock the schoolchildren of Pag-asa – some fifty of them, all in spotless white tops with green or blue skirts or shorts or brown trousers – are lined up before the

national flag. The head teacher addresses them, and then they chant and sing and raise their forearms in an oath of loyalty to their country. The ceremony serves as a stark reminder to me that I am staying not on a holiday island, but in a political hot spot.

Yesterday, I saw Chinese ships from a distance. This morning, we have been given the go-ahead to accompany the Philippine

Coastguard as they patrol their waters, ostensibly to protect their fishermen, but in reality to get as close to the Chinese ships as they dare. As far as I know it's rare for such filming to be allowed in these dangerous waters. We have an armed man aboard, wearing full combat gear. Quite what he'll be able to do if it comes to a gunfight with the Chinese I don't know, but he certainly looks intimidating: he's

one of the very few Filipinos I have encountered who hasn't returned my smile.

We pull out of the harbour, with the ship I watched the children romping on yesterday following us as our escort. Then we move slowly over the sandbank – a good fishing ground, apparently – and, in a wide arc, head towards the Chinese ships. As we approach the white vessel, the mother hen of the Chinese presence, she swings

and turns. When we set out, she was lying broadside to us. Now her bow is pointing straight at us. If she wanted to, she could crush us, and indeed I've seen photos of Chinese ships doing exactly this, and in one case actually ramming Philippine fishing boats – though I am slightly reassured when I recall that I've also seen one that showed two Chinese ships making a pincer movement to trap a Philippine fishing boat, only to miss it and ram each other.

Our captain pushes the engine up to 8 knots. We are now close enough to see that the big ship has the words 'China Coastguard', in English and Chinese, emblazoned on the side. Then two things happen. One of our crew points out a Chinese warship standing some way off and at the same time our radio crackles to life and a chillingly robotic voice warns, 'You are entering Chinese sovereign territory. Leave the area immediately.'

Our captain bobs nearer, making his territorial waters point by deliberately not turning about. The harsh voice barks out again, repeatedly commanding, 'Leave the area immediately! Leave the area immediately!'

At the same time a dinghy belonging to the Chinese ship sets out towards us, with a half-dozen figures aboard, all in orange life jackets. They are armed.

Content with our David and Goliath moment we turn and head back to Pag-asa. It's been a tense few minutes. I relax and find I've been gripping the back of the seat in front of me so hard I can still see the marks.

Back on Pag-asa, the adventure over, we seek the shade as we await the plane that will take us to Palawan again. What we have witnessed on our stay here is how fragile relations are in these waters, and how big the stakes are. The Filipinos may be on the front line, but in a sense they are no more than linesmen or referees holding back two powerful and angry teams: China and the USA. China has grand ambitions, not least the acquisition of Taiwan, which it regards as its Twenty-third Province and which lies only a few miles off the Philippines' northern border. The US is determined to resist the

fulfilment of China's ambitions, and to keep Taiwan and valuable shipping routes out of its hands. The Middle East war, which we're hearing about on the news, could be a distraction from this long-running stand-off, or it could be a spark that initiates wider conflict.

What's certainly true is that this tiny sliver of Philippine territory carries more menace than anywhere else we've been so far.

Just as we are beginning to fear another night on the floor our delayed homeward plane arrives a couple of hours late, re-fuels and loads up for the flight back. Most of the cargo is boxed and anonymous save for a half-dozen very big fish wrapped in brown paper.

At least the Chinese didn't get them.

DAY 8

★ Brooke's Point ★

LATE LAST NIGHT WE ARRIVED AT THE SOUTHERN END of Palawan, having driven for three hours from Puerto Princesa to a town called Brooke's Point. Our route passed through woods, banana and coconut plantations and paddy fields dotted with egrets and the occasional water buffalo on which the egrets perch. I love egrets: they're always looking around for a better place to stand. The water buffaloes move reassuringly slowly, like First World War tanks, allowing the egrets plenty of time to ride on their backs and extract a few insecty morsels. They both seem to embody an impression of quieter times, agricultural richness and rural harmony – of which there is plenty of evidence in southern Palawan. This part of the Philippines is largely the home of indigenous people who live, as they always have, off the generous and fertile soils.

It's also home to something commercially much more valuable. Nickel. It's the one mineral that the Philippines has in quantity, and it's in big demand internationally, for stainless steel and as an essential element of the batteries that power e-cars. Here in southern Palawan, the Ipilan Nickel Corporation has been busily extracting it, stripping away 2,800 hectares (around 4,000 football pitches' worth) of rain-forest in the process.

Its activities are clearly helping to meet a global need. They are not, however, going down well with all the locals.

We go to meet Norima, the feisty spokesperson for those opposed to nickel mining, whose family has worked the land here for generations. To reach her village, tucked away off the road, we pick our way along a perilously narrow path leading between the paddy fields before emerging into an Eden-like glade. Sunlight, flecked by the trees, falls on a settlement of stoutly built wooden cabins, which seem to be occupied largely by dogs, cats and chickens. The loudest sounds are the occasional fierce protests of a cockerel, tethered to a tree, or a passing flock of geese, squawking disapprovingly as they have to walk around us. Norima, a small, deceptively strong-willed lady of middle age, beckons me to sit at a table on her veranda.

What has aggrieved her the most, she tells me, is that the nickel company never consulted the local people or made any attempt to explain their plans when they appropriated the land high up behind the village. Now waste is present in streams coming off the mountain. Water supplies have been polluted and the stripping away of so many trees has left the mountainside more vulnerable to flooding.

There is heavy security around the recently opened mine, so she can't see what's going on. Here we are able to help, for – provided it's not spotted – we can send our drone camera up and over the mine. Norima takes us to a glade beside an old reservoir and Alex, our second cameraman, duly sends the drone up.

Norima watches the screen intently as the drone rakes the mountain and the first images are transmitted. She suddenly catches her breath and, such is the emotion at what she sees, that I realise this slightly built, tough little campaigner is wiping away a tear.

She shakes her head. 'I've never seen this before.' As the pictures come in and she sees just how much of her land has been scraped away, she gasps in increasing disbelief.

'I am sad,' she says bitterly. 'We have floods here. We have typhoons. But this is worse.'

She knows that the scar on the landscape, whose extent she has seen for the first time, will never be healed. And her reaction is one of primal despair.

It's not a feeling shared by all her neighbours. Indeed, I realise that one of her deepest regrets is that so many of them lack her visceral connection to the land. She is fundamentally opposed to what the Ipilan Nickel Corporation is doing. Large numbers of her neighbours, however, have been prepared to be bought off with such perks as new housing, a sports stadium and jobs that pay much more than traditional farming ever will.

I'm much moved by Norima and her plight. She really does care about the land that has kept her family alive for generations. They have long enjoyed a plain but idyllic existence in the woods, and now she's having to accept that their way of life will never be the same again.

We make our farewells and hit the road back to Puerto Princesa. Overnight our own bad news comes in. Five hundred Iranians and six American servicemen killed in the Middle East.

BRGY.128 ZONE-10
BOBBY HERNANE

DAY 9

Cebu

WE'RE UP EARLY TO CATCH A PLANE EAST TO CEBU, the second-largest metropolitan area in the Philippines and the capital of a group of islands known as the Visayas. Proudly named Queen City of the South, it's where Ferdinand Magellan, the first European to set foot on the Philippines, landed in 1521. He died later that year while trying to negotiate a treaty with Lapu Lapu, a local leader. Twenty years later, his fellow explorer Villalobos, who led a failed attempt to colonise the archipelago, decided to name it after the future Spanish king, Philip II. Meanwhile the Roman Catholicism that Magellan had brought with him took root and, over the following decades and centuries, grew to become the dominant religion.

There's a big party of English backpackers on the flight, and I talk to a couple from Middlesbrough who've been 'doing South-East Asia' for weeks. It strikes me that they're more travellers than holidaymakers: they may not have to face the perils that a Magellan or a Villalobos did, but their spirit of adventure and their curiosity about the world around them is the same, and I don't think it's too fanciful to see them as successors, at least in spirit, of the explorers of another age. Every single inch of the globe may now be visible at the click of a key, but if you really care about the world you have to see it with your own eyes and make your own judgements. That will inevitably involve more effort, discomfort and, possibly, risk, than surfing the internet, but it gets you away from home and out of your comfort zone.

At lunch in Cebu I am given the opportunity to sample the delicacy of the area and the nearest thing to a Philippine national dish. Vegetarians look away now. *Lechon*, roast suckling pig, is a whole pig flavoured with spices and cooked slowly over an open fire. The result, if done properly, is a thin but perfectly crispy skin covering meat that is both tender and flavoursome. It exists in various forms, and the venue where I first get to experience one of them – which is open to the street and more converted barn-like shed than restaurant – offers me *lechon kawali*, which is crispy fried pork belly. Frying proceeds apace, while waiters – all dressed in orange T-shirts and caps – shout at anyone passing to come in for the meal of a lifetime. The food is served on a scale and in a style that is distinctly industrial. *Lechon kawali*, sausages, chicken kebabs and other meaty items are brought in piled-up stacks from which I can select whatever I want. It's all done with great style and the place is packed.

Most of the diners here are much younger than I am, not least Margie de Leon, who has agreed to share the meat mountain fresh off the grill with me. She's bright, sharp and cool – a writer and a female stand-up and a savvy commentator on the world around her.

As we talk, she muses about the Roman Catholicism that Magellan brought with him to the Philippines five hundred years ago, and alights on one particular aspect of it: its attitude to divorce. The Church has always regarded marriage as a lifelong union. However, it has increasingly come to the view that, in certain circumstances, that

union can be broken. Not, however, in the Philippines. Here divorce among Roman Catholics is illegal and there is nothing that can be done about an unhappy marriage other than to endure it. Margie has first-hand experience of this. Her parents, she tells me, were utterly miserable together but not allowed to live apart. Things got better, she adds grimly, only when her father died. There is just one other place in the Roman Catholic universe where divorce is similarly shunned: the Vatican.

Doesn't she think it's time to change this?

'Of course,' she grimaces. 'Whenever I hear someone say proudly that we're the only country left in the world without divorce, I think, okay, so we're the dumbest country in the world, right?'

The law that bans divorce is so embedded that Margie thinks it stands little chance of being repealed. It's part of the country's religious and social DNA. But Margie thinks there's a degree of cynical self-interest involved, too. Men with power and money, she suggests, have the most to lose if their wives divorce them and financial settlements have to be made. For that reason alone, they're vanishingly unlikely to support reform.

In extreme circumstances, it is possible to get an annulment in the Philippines, but the process is astonishingly difficult, slow – and very expensive. 'I've had friends who've paid to have annulments, who've had to pay hundreds of thousands of pesos for it,' Margie says. She considers the practical approach adopted by other friends who are married but no longer want to be with their spouse: 'They just don't see each other any more.'

I take another mouthful of *lechon kawali*.

I mention that I've been told the only legal way to obtain a divorce in the Philippines is if it can be proved that either of the partners was insane at the time of their marriage.

Margie nods and smiles broadly at this.

We move on to other topics. I have been wondering what it's like for a woman to make her name as a comedian in a country that is – from everything I've seen so far – very conservative, and I ask Margie what her experience has been. She admits it hasn't been easy. The idea that a woman can stand up in public and make jokes doesn't sit well with many Filipinos. Criticism is widespread. Verbal attacks are common. Online trolling is a daily hazard that has to be endured. Margie describes the sinister troll farms where people can make

money from abuse (often on behalf of particular politicians) and from spreading false information (for which the powerful will pay). She herself, she says, has suffered constant abuse from these troll armies.

'I got so numb after it. And I think that in the Philippines that's what happens. We're so used to bad things happening to us that we just numb ourselves out.'

'Stand by Me' is blaring out from the restaurant speakers. Margie nods towards them. Another sign of the conservative culture that permeates everyday life in the Philippines. Twentieth-century American music is very popular – a legacy of the years when the country was an American protectorate.

And an indication of another Filipino characteristic I've noted before: their eagerness to please and to assimilate. It's part of the reason, of course, why they're so liked around the world.

As if on cue a perfect example of assimilation roars by. The jeepney, adapted from American jeeps left behind at the end of the Second World War, has become the cheap and ubiquitous transport of choice for most working Filipinos. The original framework is the same, although it often has an extended rear section where as many as are happy to squeeze in together can be seated. These days decoration is the thing: flamboyant colours, polished chrome attachments and, very often, strident religious slogans – 'Jesus saves!' 'God is with us!' One I spot coming past strikes a more contemporary, post-Covid note: 'No Face Mask, No Face Shield, No Ride!'

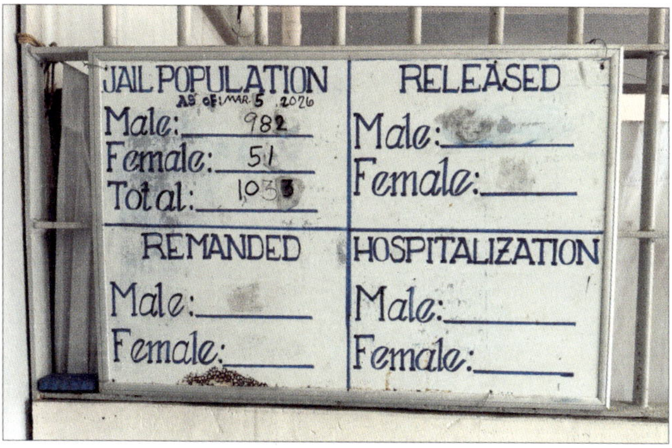

DAY 10

★ Cebu City *to* Moalboal ★

IT'S EARLY BUT THE STREETS ARE ALREADY BUSY AS WE climb up a steep hill towards the CPDRC – the Cebu Provincial Detention and Rehabilitation Center. It's not exactly a prison; more a holding centre for those waiting to have their cases heard. Such is the snail-like pace of the Philippine justice system that some have been confined here for months, even years, so adding to the burdens of one of the most overcrowded prison systems in the world.

Here in Cebu a group of remand officers came up with an idea to relieve some of the growing tension in an institution where so many inmates had so little space. Something that would make the spacious courtyard more than just an assembly arena. What they produced would unwittingly propel this detention centre to national stardom.

We're received like visiting royalty by the staff, who have placed a white plastic chair for me on a balcony overlooking the courtyard so that I can have a bird's-eye view. I feel embarrassingly conspicuous, as if reprising my portrayal of Pontius Pilate in the film *Life of Brian*. Below me, and on the far side of the yard, detainees are beginning to appear. They all wear the standard-issue orange overalls. The staff are distinguished by their bluey-grey tops. Morning prayers are delivered over a booming loudspeaker and the national anthem is played.

Then the show we've come all this way to see gets under way.

Music starts and the three hundred or so inmates taking part begin to move and circle and swing and strut in perfect time. Their moves are coordinated with a precision you only otherwise see at the slickest pop concert. A core group of very smart, athletic dancers leads

the performance and keeps up the energy levels, but all those involved know how to move together and sing together, and nobody flags in the half-hour of breathtakingly exciting performance that follows.

When they finish, chests heaving, arms thrown in the air, the applause from our small number of privileged spectators is long and sustained. I find it hard to take in the fact that all these dancers – men and women – who have made us all feel so exhilarated are not themselves free, and that after this powerful show they must go back to crowded cells, clutching for hope at any rumours of when their cases might be heard. Glenn, the choreographer of this sensational spectacle, is an inmate himself. He's been here nine years.

12
12 ARYIE

13

HOT GARLIC FLAVOR
NOW TASTIER & CRUNCHIER
Sweet Chili
CORN CHIPS
BBQ FLAVOR
Jaywen
THIS SIDE UP

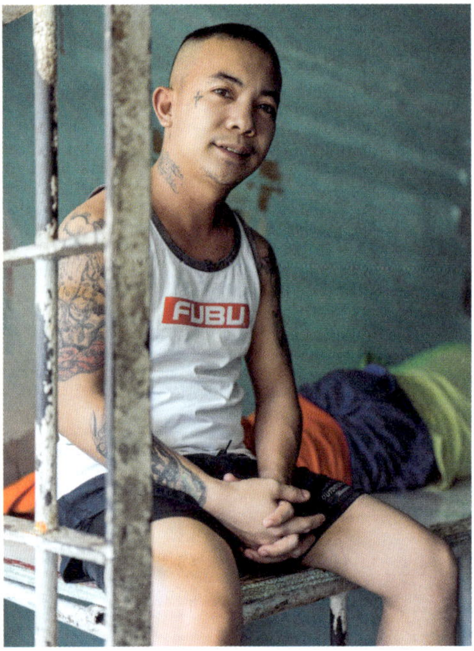

Before we leave, I'm taken around to meet some of the inmates in their cells. There could hardly be a greater contrast with what we've just seen. Some of the cells, or detainment areas, are little more than long, thin rooms with bunks down both sides, and a small area for preparing food and drinks. Into this space up to fifteen people are squeezed together for most of the day and night. The prison official who accompanies me round makes no attempt to disguise the conditions. He remembers a time when there were so many in a cell there was standing room only. I assume he must be pulling my leg, but, incredibly, I don't think he was.

I talk to a man called Joshua – short, stocky and smiling. He's awaiting trial for 'frustrated murder'. Basically that means a murder that didn't come off. He's remarkably cheerful.

He points out that dance is not just for those who want to express themselves. It's compulsory, as are the football and basketball and exercise regimes that the centre organises.

What I've seen today is the brilliant and the desperate, side by side. In their bid to keep this place tranquil, officers and inmates have come up with an activity that everyone in the Philippines

now knows about. But it hasn't helped anyone's case to go through any faster.

As a way of thanking the inmates for the display they've laid on for us we have purchased *lechon* for them all. Ten suckling pigs are brought in one by one. Each receives a great ovation from unseen voices in the cell blocks that line the courtyard.

We've spent the morning exploring one serious challenge that the Philippines faces: overcrowded detention centres and prisons and the painfully slow progress of the justice system. This afternoon we move on to investigate another problem – or perhaps, more accurately – a potentially existential threat. The whole world is familiar with the concept of climate change. Here in the Philippines, though, its impact is no abstract notion. It's an ever-present reality. Rising sea

levels threaten the future of many of the over seven thousand islands that make up the archipelago, while extreme weather conditions are a constant hazard. Hence the Evacuation Centres I have noticed in Pag-asa and elsewhere, and the evacuation instructions posted in every town and village.

We drive to the neighbourhood of Talisay in Cebu City. Here, just three months before our arrival, downpours from Typhoon Tino caused the Mananga river to swell so fast that flood-control walls, put in place at great expense less than ten years earlier, were not just surmounted, they were torn apart. From a mercifully spared road bridge above the river, I look down on the destruction of what was, until so recently, a vibrant and bustling area. Concrete embankments have been broken and twisted like putty. Houses belonging to the

poorest and most vulnerable have been smashed to pieces and tossed aside like discarded boxes. Even the more solid industrial buildings have split walls and collapsed roofs.

Dozens of lives were lost along the river.

As I walk down among the wreckage I encounter Veronica Sordilla, a mother and grandmother in her late fifties whose house was swept away in the devastation wrought by the typhoon. The warning of the impending flood came at five in the morning, she tells me, but although she was able to escape with thirteen of her family, there was no time to grab any possessions. She was forced to spend two weeks at a government evacuation centre which she found dirty and uncomfortable. Then she asked to be allowed to go home again.

Arguably, she is one of the more fortunate, in that she has been provided with a hastily repaired temporary home. But there is little evidence of other repairs being made along the riverside, and if the

collapsed defences are not restored before the rains recur, then the nightmarish events visited on her and her community could happen all over again. To that extent, her return home may prove to be less a cause for celebration, more a stay of execution.

As so often with natural disasters, there's a depressingly man-made aspect to all this. It has emerged recently that multi-billion-dollar contracts to build barriers and flood defences across the country were awarded corruptly, and that the work was then done on the cheap and in the wrong places. A number of politicians and company directors are therefore now facing lawsuits, as commentators muse on how little seems to have changed since the cronyism, cover-ups and waste of public money of the Marcos years. Now, of course, there's another Marcos at the helm. It strikes me that he has his work cut out if he wants to ensure that the big, much-lauded, highly expensive flood defence programmes that are now being touted are watertight, literally and morally.

We're staying tonight at a quiet hotel in the town of Moalboal. Good food, well-kept gardens overflowing with frangipani, hibiscus and bougainvillea. A much-appreciated few hours of relaxation before an arduous day tomorrow when I shall take part in what sounds like something we could have written for *Monty Python*. Swimming with sardines.

DAY 11

★ Moalboal ★

IN MY MIND, SARDINES ARE GENERALLY ASSOCIATED with tins and toast. But in the Philippines they are a tourist attraction. Off the coast at Moalboal millions of little silvery fish gather in shoals which move en masse and in strict formation. Marine biologists have no explanation for this phenomenon other than that, if all move together, individuals are less vulnerable. Collective security. Be that as it may, the crowds are already gathering by the time we arrive at the beach to film my participation in what the tourist brochures call the Sardine Run. As one who loves sardines and fish-slapping, how could I resist?

It's one thing to swim with the sardines. It's a whole other thing to be filmed doing it, as I very quickly learn. A professional called Gladys, who, as part of her day job, teaches people to be mermaids, is on hand to make sure that I'm in the right place at the right time. Once I'm in the right place at the right time, she tells me, I will be filmed from below by our underwater camerawoman Beyoncé (no relation) as I glide in harmony with my fishy friends. What could possibly go wrong?

Many things, as it turns out.

A prime section of the beach has been cordoned off for our exclusive use, and expectant sardinophiles have to wait to one side, entertained only by my undignified attempts to enter the water over the rocks.

'On your bottom, Michael,' our director calls out helpfully. 'Backwards!' Good advice as it turns out, but not what a deeply confused eighty-two-year-old, carrying flippers, and wearing punishingly tight goggles, wants to hear on a specially cleared beach.

Once in the water I'm given mixed signals. Some people are trying to stop me drowning; others are trying to get me lined up for a spectacular shot with a million sardines.

Another complication is that the ocean current has strengthened and the shoal has been swept beyond the stretch of water we first enter. They have clearly not been told to stay within the area specially reserved for filming.

Then comes a miraculous moment. Having sorted out my breathing, cleared water from my face mask, avoided swallowing my snorkel and discovered that the sweep of the waves is filtering out

the various shouted instructions, I am able to look around me and, for a brief moment, be on my own. Except I'm not. Sweeping below me, twisting and turning in a mass of glittering silver, are the sardines. There are so many of them swimming in such perfectly held formation that they look almost impermeable, like a wall – a wall rising and falling and turning and swooping with lyrical smoothness. My only regret is that I can't dive deep enough to join them. But I know now what all the fuss is about. It's been worth enduring any number of indignities to witness something so majestic and so soothing at the same time.

Once out of the water, dry but still in a state of some elation, I take to the road again, as we retrace our steps back over the bridge to Cebu City. We've just been to look at food from the sea; now we're going to look at food from the land.

Just outside Moalboal we stop at a small plantation where coconuts are being collected in the old way. Raffy, probably in his thirties, lithe and nimble, shins – quite unaided – up the swaying trunk of a coconut palm. The coconuts are anything from sixty to a hundred feet up and when he reaches them he must disengage one of his hands to twist the coconut pods until one falls to the ground. A picture of confident ease, he is back down in what seems seconds. He cracks open a coconut with his machete and we all take a swig of the highly nutritious liquid inside.

The Philippines produces more coconuts than anywhere else in the world, though no one seems to know what proportion of them are still picked by hand and whether there are many people left with Raffy's extraordinary climbing skills. Impressive as it looks, it's a hard way to make a living, and Raffy and his family, I learn, are some of the poorest on the island.

It's a three-hour drive to our home for the night, along a road packed with towns and villages merging one into the other. It's in such extended urban areas, around Manila and here in Cebu, that I feel the reality of a statistic that so surprised me when I first came across it – that the Philippines has the seventh-largest population in Asia (and the fourteenth largest in the world).

I find myself missing the tranquillity of Palawan, where very few seem to live.

WASH
MALABANAN
SIP-SIP
POZO NEGRO
DECLOGGING
0955 123 0609
0909 950 8617

DAY 13

To Davao City

WE'VE JUST ENJOYED A REFRESHING DAY OFF ON Mactan Island, which lies across the water from Cebu City. The suburb in which we stayed is called Lapu Lapu, and is named after the local leader Ferdinand Magellan encountered when he arrived in the Philippines in 1521. Infuriated by Magellan's demands for tribute and for the recognition of the King of Spain as his overlord, Lapu Lapu engaged the invading Spanish force in battle and quickly overwhelmed them, killing Magellan and several of his men in the process.

These days, they're making a big effort to entice tourists here but it's all rather cart before the horse in that ambition has clearly run ahead of infrastructure. Big hotels have been built side by side off what is little more than a country lane. The main street of the town is permanently jammed as work goes on to provide access for all the anticipated extra traffic. Progress is limited at some junctions by interminably long lights. Some have countdowns that begin at two hundred.

Fortunately, we've been warned about the traffic situation and have taken the precaution of making an early start. It pays off. We reach Mactan airport in plenty of time and set off for our next destination, Davao, on schedule.

Beside me on the hour-and-a-half flight is a seventy-one-year-old Australian surfer. He loves the Philippines, he tells me, adding with a hint of pride that he's broken two ribs surfing here in the last two months. Apparently he makes his own boards and is off to Davao City to meet his girlfriend. A happy man.

Davao is effectively the gateway to the island of Mindanao, and despite its sprawling population of around two million is generally regarded as the cleanest and safest city in the Philippines. Outside Davao things are more problematic. While much of the population of Mindanao as a whole is Roman Catholic, South Mindanao is predominantly Muslim, and tensions between the two communities, which stretch back to the Marcos era and before, have now reached the point where the UK Foreign Office has declared half the island a red zone – effectively off limits to British would-be visitors.

Davao itself has not been free from either violence or controversy. By the 1970s it had become a hotbed of political, religious and ethnic tensions. Crime was a serious problem. Then in 1988 a new mayor of Davao was elected who vowed to bring the city to heel. His name was Rodrigo Duterte.

After a very good lunch at the Mixed Temptation Chinese restaurant I meet up with Kookie de Leon, a writer about politics and families (she's forty-eight and has four grandchildren) and an unapologetic Duterte supporter. Powerful memories have shaped her world view. When she was five, a terrorist bomb exploded during Easter worship at Davao's main cathedral, killing or injuring large numbers of people. Blamed on Islamic terrorists, it proved to be the first in a wave of similar, if less destructive, attacks. Gang violence also spiralled, to the point where, as a child, Kookie was warned by her parents that the streets of Central Davao, which we are walking now, were completely off limits to her.

She's at pains to point out how quickly things changed when Rodrigo Duterte became mayor. 'Under his leadership Davao became safer in ways ordinary people could feel immediately,' she says. She describes how his firm control of the city, and his insistence on very strict boundaries for gangs running drugs or trafficking young girls for sex, made the city safe for her children to a degree that would have been unthinkable when she was their age. Her support for Duterte is calm and unlaced with any political venom.

I press her on the issue of his notorious use of 'death squads' – responsible, among many other deaths, for that of Emily Soriano's son Angelito in Manila. There's no getting away from police figures of six thousand dead in this extra-legal drug war (human rights groups suggest up to thirty thousand), and Duterte certainly hasn't helped his defence case at the International Criminal Court by previously boasting on television that he himself had killed drug dealers and addicts.

Kookie nods a little wearily as if she's had to confront these uncomfortable facts before. Her response is essentially that those who never knew the lawlessness and urban violence in the city prior to 'Digong' – as Duterte is popularly known – beginning his clean-up cannot begin to understand how great a change for the better he initiated. She admits that some of his actions were clearly against the law, but argues that the charges he faces are disproportionate and the emotive phrase 'death squads' exaggerated. She suggests that right and wrong are not absolutes. And she sighs with impatience at the International Criminal Court's case against him.

'Digong operated in an environment shaped by decades of violence, insurgency and drug proliferation.' What, she asks, does a court ten thousand miles away know about *sawplat* – the street name for young girls selling their bodies for meth? 'These things won't disappear through moral declarations,' she argues.

Kookie is bright and intelligent, and having to explain to an outsider why she feels positive about Duterte clearly frustrates her. I also know that she's not a lone voice. Duterte's eightieth birthday on 28 March 2025 – just days after he was ambushed at Manila airport and flown to the Netherlands – was celebrated by thousands in Davao, who took to the streets to protest against his arrest. In Manila, meanwhile, police blocked a convoy of a hundred motorbike riders, who were blasting out music and holding posters that carried the same blunt message: 'Bring Him Home'. Barely two months later the now incarcerated Duterte was re-elected mayor of Davao by a landslide.

Davao may be cleaner and tidier than Manila but I'm pleased to discover that it's not entirely strait-laced. Back in the early 2000s a dance craze known as Budots took root here, and thanks to the enthusiasm of a local DJ, Sherwin Tuna (who goes by the name of 'DJ Love'), it rapidly swept through social media and far beyond the shores of the Philippines. *Budots* is street slang for slackers or drug addicts – those outside society – and the dance that it inspired is suitably grungy.

I am introduced to it by the man who brought it to the wider world. Slightly to my surprise, given his success, the now forty-nine-year-old DJ Love lives and works in a cave-like studio located in a warren of dark passageways, in a ramshackle complex that houses over a hundred families. A huge computer shares space with plates of half-eaten food waiting to be washed up at a sink. Somehow it all seems an appropriate setting for a dance that was born in the poorest parts of the city.

DAY 13

DJ Love takes me outside to where a group of schoolgirls has gathered at the corner of the street to perform the dance for us. They're wearing T-shirts and ripped shorts. The dance is deliberately provocative and the music is hard and harsh, with a lot of sharp scratchy breaks. Prominent among the moves is a gun-to-the-head finger movement. DJ Love explains that the message is that drugs can kill you, but watching the girls twerk and twist on a street corner in Davao, I can't help feeling that what I'm seeing here is less of a condemnation and more of a celebration of the wild and uncontrollable side of life.

est Dried Fish from Bantayan Island, Cebu, Philippines
FISH BONES
100 grams
Consume on or before 12 AUG 2026

EST. 2020
BAI BUWAD
SPECIAL PUSIT 100G
CEBU'S BEST DRIED DANGGIT AND PU

DABOY
PURO Pork Belly
CHILI-CIOUS TALAGA!!!

Dried Fish from Bantayan Island, Ce
ISALTED BONELESS D
100 grams
Consume on or before 24 AUG

Lumpiang "Isda" 10
LUMPIANG TOGUE
GULAY - 10

Sasas

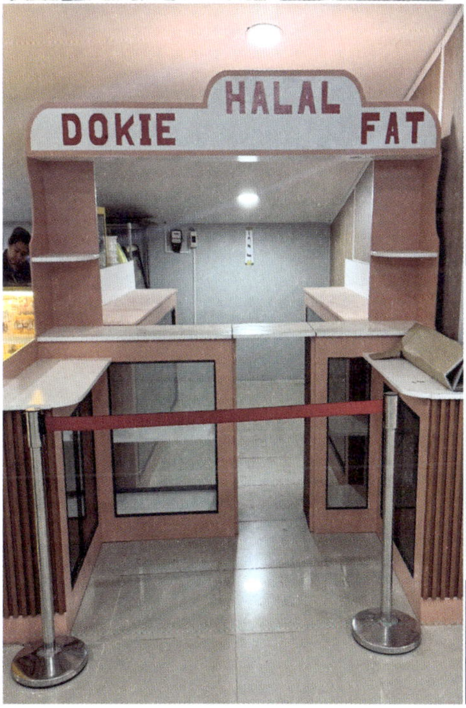
DOKIE
HALAL
FAT

24/7
COFFEE
THE ROBOT BARISTA
What's your nickname & email?
STEP 2
Add your nickname and email address
SCAN QR CODE TO COLLECT DRINK >>>

DAY 14

Davao *to* Marawi

TODAY WE'RE HEADING NORTH-WEST TO ONE OF THE most troubled areas of the Philippines. Back in 2017 the city of Marawi was partially destroyed by Islamist extremists in the course of a five-month siege that the rest of the world barely noticed.

Another long drive, and the weather's on the turn. Darkening skies. At Tugbok, not far out of Davao, we stop to try one of the area's most popular and controversial fruits, the durian. It's about the size of a coconut, with a pointy, prickly shell, and when sliced open it gives off a distinctively pungent aroma. Some can deal with it, but Girlie really can't bear it. She doesn't hold back. To her, durian smells of vomit and drains.

Many hotels and airlines defer to the Girlies of this world and refuse to stock the fruit, but here, by the roadside, a lady has rows and rows prominently displayed.

A black limousine purrs to a halt while we're tasting and a lady of some means steps out of a door held open for her by her chauffeur. She appraises the durians with imperious care before nodding to her driver, who proceeds to load boxes of them into her car.

Having lost my sense of smell some years ago I'm not really in a position to judge just how virulent durians are. As for the crew, their reactions range from favourable to appalled, although no one catches a hint of either vomit or drains among the subtle flavours.

What I can taste and enjoy greatly is a mangosteen, a much smaller and more flavourful fruit just coming into season and piled nearby. Described as the 'Queen of Fruits' it's about the size of a passion fruit and quite delicious, with a sweet, slightly sharp bite – enough to get through to my taste buds which, unlike my nasal detectors, are still working fine.

We drive on. For some reason I never expected the Philippines to contain so much high ground, but at one point, when we emerge from the trees and reach the forecourt of the Zig-Zag View Café, we find a magnificent vista opening up before us. A terrace with tables and chairs promises a break where we can enjoy a panorama of green and pleasant land rolling away into the far distance. Frustratingly, the café is closed.

By mid-afternoon we are, quite suddenly, into a very different environment from anything we've seen so far. As if to herald the change, it starts to rain for the first time since we arrived in the Philippines. Tentatively at first, then increasingly heavily. The human landscape changes, too. We spot mosques in the villages through which we pass. In the streets women are wearing the hijab and chador. I glance at the Foreign Office travel advice map we've brought with us. The area we are in now is coloured red and marked 'Advise against all travel'.

The first military checkpoints we've seen on our journey start emerging out of the rain. Then, a few miles from Marawi, we're brought to a halt at a red 'Stop' barrier. We're told that we can progress no further until the authorities are able to organise a military escort to take us into the city. The rain patters on the roof of our vehicle as the paperwork is done. We and our vehicles are photographed. Preceded by armed soldiers in the back of a pickup truck, we finally head on down the road into Marawi.

It may be perceived as a high-risk area, but the streets look lively enough. It's Ramadan and people are out breaking their fast and preparing evening meals.

At the Marawi Ranaw Business Hotel, I am given a huge room with a lounge area, two capacious beds and a bathroom so tiny I can barely get my whole body into the shower. But after our long drive I don't require much apart from dinner and alcohol. Dinner is fine; alcohol is not available. Finally, I return to my palatial room. The lighting proves to be eccentric. Ultimately the only way I can find to switch off lots of unnecessary strip lighting is to turn everything off at the mains.

The rain lashes against the windows as I try to decide which of the massive beds to sleep in. Having made my choice, I feel like Tom Thumb as I climb aboard and ease myself into a sea of pillows.

DAY 15

Marawi

THERE HAS BEEN A STRONG MUSLIM PRESENCE IN THE southern Philippines since the fourteenth century, when Islam spread to the region from what are now Indonesia and the islands of Malaysia, and trade between Mindanao and its Muslim neighbours thrived.

Things started to change once the Spanish took control. Now Christianity became the dominant religion, and as Manila evolved into an ever more important trading hub and the north became richer, so the south was left behind. After Spain ceded control of the archipelago to the US in 1898, the Philippines' new American overlords encouraged Christians to settle in Mindanao – a policy that in various forms continued after the Philippines gained its independence in

1946. For their part, the Muslims of the south – known since Spanish colonial times as Moros – came to resent their non-Muslim rulers, and at various points in their history have engaged in an armed struggle against them.

In May 2017 security forces raided premises on the outskirts of Marawi to serve an arrest warrant on Isnilon Hapilon, the leader of Abu Sayyaf, a Jihadist group linked to ISIS, whose avowed objective was to set up an Islamic state in Mindanao. The search became a skirmish and several people were killed on both sides, including Hapilon's wife and one of his children, although he himself escaped. The situation then escalated. Dozens of Abu Sayyaf fighters poured into the streets of Marawi to launch an all-out assault they had clearly been planning for some time. Their initial target was the banking and commercial district, the heart of the city's wealth.

The police were taken by surprise at the intensity and efficiency of the attack. By the time they had grasped the scale of what was happening, Abu Sayyaf had occupied a number of buildings in the city centre, and declared the city of Marawi the Muslim-only capital of a new Islamic state. What followed was a bitterly fought battle between Abu Sayyaf and government forces that went on for five months and resulted in the deaths of hundreds of people.

Even now, nearly ten years after the end of the battle of Marawi, much of the centre of the city remains in ruins. It's still widely referred to as 'Ground Zero'.

This is where we are heading this grey and damp morning, with mist shrouding the mountains north of the city and more rain expected.

As we and our armed escort cross a bridge in the middle of town, we reach the beginning of Ground Zero. On one side of the river stands a smart hotel, a symbol of the recently attempted regeneration of the city. Elsewhere down by the waterside, where some rebuilding has been going on in an area called Rizal Park, a big wheel, silent and still, awaits the first passenger of the day. On the other side of the river, however, houses and half-demolished buildings stand empty, their roofs open to the sky, holes gashed in their blackened walls. Much of the destruction is in an area that runs parallel to a lake, so creating a jarring contrast between an almost Swiss-like landscape and a war zone.

We pull up at a crossroads where a number of once impressive, now wrecked buildings linger on. Most striking of these is a large mosque that is completely hollowed out. My first thought is that it seems so pointless that Jihadists should have destroyed a mosque in a city they wanted as a Muslim capital. Then I consider that most of the destruction in this siege would have been the work of government forces as they tried to flush out those Jihadists. For the people who lived here and loved their city the siege must have been doubly unendurable as they watched their finest buildings being destroyed by those who were supposed to be protecting them.

We carry on up a steep hill to inspect a stretch of upmarket offices and houses built for the wealthy of Marawi. All have handsome frontages, behind some of which fine tiling and stucco decorations can be seen. One particularly fine porchway wall has 'ISIS' painted across it. At the bottom of the road a wanted poster with photos of the perpetrators flaps in a sharp breeze. Apart from their leader, Usman, they all look like children.

According to Drieza, a local community leader who lived through it all, many of the inhabitants here were convinced that the siege would be over in a few days. They therefore left their houses on the assumption that they would be able to come back after the weekend, when it was all over. They have never returned.

As there's no one around to stop me, I decide to enter the impressive shell of a solid-looking five-storey building and climb up wide, rubble-strewn stairways through rooms which obviously saw fighting. I note the classic sign of siege warfare: holes punched through the interior walls to allow the besieged to move from room to room without being seen at the windows. I observe, too, the sad

signs of human loss. Cups, plates, a child's shoes lying in the dust, delicately painted tiles chosen so carefully for a bathroom, now split and chipped. Plans shattered. Fine rooms stripped of their dignity.

As I re-emerge a woman living opposite tells me that the building I've just walked through – a mix of apartments and a hotel – had been completed only a few months before it was attacked.

She nods sadly. 'And it had a lovely view of the lake.'

Only one in ten of the fourteen thousand people whose houses were damaged or destroyed in the siege have received compensation. One of the lucky few is Queenie, who was able to move into a smart new house a year or two ago where she now lives with her ten-year-old son. To give me some idea of what life was like before the fighting, she takes me to see the school where she was once a pupil.

We have to scramble up an overgrown bank of tall grasses to get to the entrance hall. Insurgents installed themselves here, and there must have been a fierce battle to get them out. The walls are covered in bullet holes and shrapnel scars, the floor piled with rubbish. Bits of collapsed roof block the way out into the schoolyard. The silence is eerie. Beneath an arch the word 'Library' is rather elegantly picked out. There are, of course, no books to be seen.

I felt very strongly the stifling of life here. This was a school. These buildings would once have overflowed with voices.

Queenie is at pains to point out that when she was here most of the teachers were Christian. Back then, she says, there was mutual tolerance and a desire for co-existence between Muslims and Christians, which was completely at odds with Abu Sayyaf's determination to provoke a Holy War and then create a city exclusively for Muslims.

In a lane outside she points to a line of empty buildings with trees which sprouted inside now growing out through their roofs. These, she tells me, were the shops where they would go for pastries after school. Now all that stands here by way of hope for the future is a sign for a water sterilisation scheme financed by UK Aid.

The rain has started again as I say goodbye to Queenie at the door of her new house. I'm glad I've met her. She is positive and articulate, and through her I've learnt a bit more about how people survive appalling tragedy. The role model for her stoicism is her father. When the fighting broke out, she tells me, he made sure that Queenie and the rest of the family were taken to safety, but decided to remain behind in the house that he had helped build even as battles raged in the streets around him and supplies were cut off. It was seventeen days before they could rescue him. Though he's been dead some years now, Queenie talks of him with real emotion. Not sadness, but pride.

The disruption of life that the five-month siege caused will mark not only this generation but generations to come. Thousands of people who lost their houses are still in displacement camps, dotted about the city. If the government continues to make replacement of services rather than housing a priority, they will have to remain there for years more. We pass one such camp on the way back to our hotel. Row upon row of identical grey bungalows rising up a hill.

Next year their occupants will have been living in temporary accommodation for a decade.

SAUDI BOY
BARBER SHOP

DAY 16

Marawi *to* Zamboanga

TODAY WE CONTINUE OUR JOURNEY THROUGH THE Foreign Office's red zone. If all goes smoothly we will take a ferry down the Sulu archipelago to the troubled island of Jolo, close to the most southerly point of the Philippines. By then we'll be eight hundred miles from Manila – and less than two hundred from Malaysia.

First, though, our longest road trip of the journey. To get from Marawi to the ferry port at Zamboanga will take us most of the day. Low cloud girdles the mountains, and rain doesn't seem far off as we make our way out of this bruised and battered city, past the tyre depots and the building sites.

Recycled car tyres are a prominent feature of roadside life throughout the Philippines. Many small towns and villages use them to beautify their verges. The tyres are painted in vibrant colours – deep purple, lemon, green, pink – and are often filled with earth and used as planters. I've noticed there is some competition between communities as to who can create the most eye-catching. Those with a plentiful supply of used tyres will stack them three or four high. It's a simple way of recycling a lot of rubber, and beautifying and tidying the place up at the same time.

A few miles beyond Marawi we say goodbye to our military escort, and the atmosphere becomes a little more relaxed. I notice, as we weave our way through the mountains, that substantial work is going on to reinforce the steep sides of the road, but embankments cleared of soil-securing trees and not yet stabilised with nets or concrete look lethal to me. And indeed at one point all traffic on

our busy road grinds to a halt for almost an hour. The recent heavy rains have caused a landslide ahead.

Delayed but not defeated, we stop for lunch in the town of Pagadian. Its urban buzz comes as a bit of a shock after landslides and mountain roads, but at least we're able to track down something to eat at Jollibee in the Robinsons Pagadian mall. Jollibee does good fast food for a predominantly young clientele, and this branch is busy and noisy, even though it's still Ramadan. The brand is simple. Light, bright, shiny-clean premises serving light, bright, shiny-clean food like chicken and spaghetti with Philippine sauces. For some reason Jollibee, like that other Philippine brand, San Miguel beer, has become an international success story. The flagship Jollibee in London is prominently located in Leicester Square.

By now a degree of anxiety is creeping in. The landslide delay and a long lunch break have squeezed the time left to complete the rest of today's journey. Our ferry to the Sulu islands doesn't leave until nine o'clock tonight, but there's some way to go, and when we arrive at the port we still have to check in and get our tickets. If we don't make it, then a large portion of our final day's filming will have to be completely reorganised.

Eventually we're out of the mountains and onto the plain. A pale yellow sun reflects back from paddy fields as we pass through various outlying villages. As it finally sets we're in the busy streets of Zamboanga. We grab a quick meal, as there will be no food on the overnight ferry, then race to the port, much relieved that, after all our adventures, we've arrived at the dockside a whole hour ahead of the scheduled departure time.

At 11.30 we're still at the dockside. No one seems to know quite why. Our director, Neil, surmises that it could have something to do with safety checks, pointing out that only a month ago a ferry on this same run sank off Basilan, an island just south of Zamboanga. Sixty-five people died and fourteen were unaccounted for. I made the mistake of checking the details on CNN's website a little earlier and wish I hadn't.

'Sea accidents are common in the Philippine archipelago,' I read, 'because of frequent storms, badly maintained vessels, overcrowding and spotty enforcement of safety regulations.' The article went on to remind me that the world's worst peacetime ferry disaster took

place in the central Philippines in December 1987, when more than 4,300 lives were lost.

I realise I must stop fretting as, under the critical eye of the coastguards, the rear loading ramp is raised then lowered yet again and various vehicles offloaded and repositioned. Last month's capsize was blamed on poor distribution of the ship's load. The ferry company responsible for the accident has just lost its licence. Understandably, this new operator is being extra careful.

Conditions onboard are spartan, the sleeping arrangements consisting of nothing more than a network of steel-framed double bunks that are spread across the ship's two decks. No bedding is

provided. I am lucky in that Girlie and Maki have done their best to create a first-class feel to our sleeping area by supplying thin, colour-coordinated mattresses and pillows. Most of our fellow passengers, however, just stretch out to sleep in their working clothes. The majority of those on our deck are young Muslim women.

By the time the tow ropes are released it's getting on for three hours past our scheduled departure time. I'm dimly aware of the ship pushing slowly and smoothly away from the dockside. I register the quiet movement of the waves and sink happily back to sleep.

An hour later I'm awake again. Conditions have changed. A brisk wind is hitting our starboard side and I feel the ship begin to pitch and roll. Moments later she crests a wave and comes down so heavily on the other side that all I can hear is the rumbling of dozens of wheeled suitcases as they race down the gangways, to a chorus of screams from their owners.

As they chase after them there is a brief moment when time stands still, and then MV *Maria Rebecca* mounts another wave and they all roll back again.

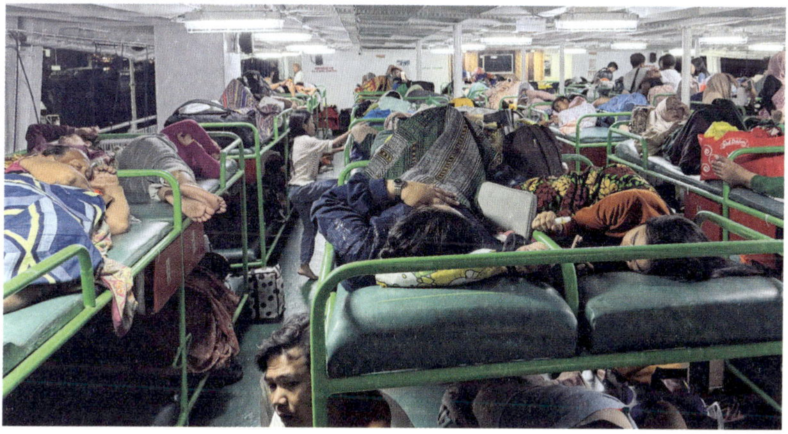

DAY 17

Jolo

WOKEN BY A STIFF BREEZE OFF THE SEA, I LOOK AROUND me. All our young fellow passengers have donned life jackets during the night and are lying bulkily on their bunks.

I get up as dawn breaks. Fortunately, I don't have to dress as I never undressed, so I stand at the deck-rail and watch the sea rising and falling, and a spectacular sunrise slowly emerging. Even after so many travels I'm still mesmerised by the play of light on the surface of the water. And the slow reveal of a rising sun is supremely calming.

In the distance I can just make out the dim shapes of rocky islands. We shall be spending the day on Jolo, the largest island of the Sulu archipelago, and potentially the most dangerous stopping-off point on our journey. It's been an Abu Sayyaf stronghold for some years and has gained a reputation for kidnappings and general violence. Seven years ago a Catholic church on the island was bombed. At least twenty-two people died in the blast.

A more reassuring picture of Jolo emerges from a quietly articulate fellow passenger with whom I strike up a conversation. He was born and brought up on Jolo. I learn that he teaches journalism, and that he has just been to Zamboanga with some of his students to compete in a debating competition. Apparently, they came seventh, which makes him very proud as educational facilities on Jolo are quite basic. His view of his home island is a cautiously optimistic one. There may have been problems in the past, he says, but now things are much better and safer. He's happy to be going home.

He must have told some of his students what I'm doing here, because one of them comes up to me as we approach the port, and asks, very respectfully, if I could tell him the three most important things that would make him a good writer. Story, story, story, story, I tell him. He nods slowly and moves away. I know what he's thinking. This man can't count.

Eventually Jolo town comes in sight, its skyline dominated by a handsome white mosque, with minarets at all four corners, that shines in the early-morning sunshine. Since we're only going to be here for a day, we're keen to get on with things, but that proves rather easier said than done. From the moment MV *Maria Rebecca* drops her loading ramp and the luggage-laden passengers start disembarking, just as many people pour the other way: relatives, freelance porters, boys begging, all pushing their way up the precipitous steel ladders and merging chaotically with those coming down. Ahead of us, a pickup truck backs up to the ramp. A body wrapped in a white shroud is lifted out from the hold, carried through the crowd of disembarking passengers and laid in the back. Keening relatives

squeeze in around it. Petals are scattered and scents sprinkled. The truck then moves away, very slowly, through the swirling crowd.

By the time we ourselves have managed to disembark, we're hours behind schedule. We grab a speedy breakfast and take a swift shower at a local hotel, then move quickly to our next destination, where I am hoping I will be able to meet up with a former member of Abu Sayyaf, the Jihadist group that has given Jolo such a feared reputation. His name is Javer Asara Latip, and rumour has it that he has come to some agreement with the army whereby they leave him in peace and he helps them out in some undefined way.

We drive out of Jolo town with an armed escort, past a military checkpoint, and then down a long estate road through banana and coconut plantations and pleasantly sheltered farmland. Eventually, we pull up at a place called Talipao which, with its open-sided, timber-framed, thatched-roofed huts, looks like something out of a children's

story. A folksy wooden sign close by advertises 'Horse Back Riding'. There's nothing here in the slightest bit threatening.

On the other side of the road, set discreetly behind a hedge and well-kept garden, is the house where Javer and his family live.

Whether it's just for show or whether it's because some threat really does lurk here in this idyllic setting, our escort draw their rifles and fan out beneath the trees.

Girlie goes into the house and there is some negotiating.

Finally, Javer emerges, wearing a white T-shirt, dark-blue cotton shorts and sandals. He has olive-coloured skin, a black goatee beard and black hair secured in a knot behind his head. It's hard to pinpoint his age, but I guess that he's in his late forties. He looks in good shape. I can't help noticing that the first thing he does when he comes out is to give the leader of our military escort a big hug. Girlie introduces me to him. He responds with a polite but guarded smile. We shake hands.

A group of locals stand around watching – older men, who clearly carry less authority. They seem to relate to him as a backing group would to a lead singer. They hover as we decide where best to conduct the interview but they don't seem to be hostile. Eventually Javer and I opt to sit side by side on a wooden bench in the hut.

My immediate impression of him is that he is soft-spoken and disarming. But I must beware of being too easily charmed. Javer was a member of Abu Sayyaf for twenty years, during which time he and his fellow members wreaked pain and suffering on the people of Jolo and on visiting Westerners as the group strove, often with violence, to achieve their goal of a Muslim conquest of the Sulu islands.

He speaks via an interpreter, neither imploring my understanding nor hectoring me with justifications. I learn that he was only ten years old when he joined Abu Sayyaf and that he grew up protected and educated by the older men in the group. He respected them, he says, and came to believe in the justice of the holy war they were pursuing, a war in which there would have to be casualties, even though he claims never to have killed anyone himself. Whatever the truth of his assertion, the fact remains that he stayed with Abu Sayyaf for twenty years, and that during that time he worked his way up to become the leader of a group dedicated to the forcible takeover of the Sulu islands.

Now, however, he has renounced violence and, he says, made his peace with the people around him.

I ask him whether, had we met twenty years ago, he would have wanted to kill me. It's not a question he was expecting, and for a moment he is fazed by it. Then he sort of shakes his head and dismisses such a notion with – of all things – a smile.

He comes across as a clever, charismatic man – guarded at the beginning of our conversation; slightly more relaxed by the end. He sounds humble. He may possibly be a little contrite. Interestingly, after his interpreter has left, I discover that he understands a lot more English than he wanted us to know.

He points out his son, a lanky teenager on a bike, watching what's going on. Javer's wife appears with some other women who lay out elaborate refreshments on the table. It could be tea with the vicar.

As we drive back to Jolo, I'm left with conflicting views. Clearly the ex-Jihadist was happy to talk to us, although he had no real need to. So was he setting the record straight? Was he hoping to gain some prestige from the media exposure? Or was he playing with us, pitting his wits against ours – employing the skills that took him to the top of a feared terrorist group to show he still had it?

I've always been wary of such labels as 'Good' and 'Bad', 'Terrorist' and 'Freedom fighter'. They never tell you anything approaching the full story. For that you need to go to the source, meet the people on the ground, look at the context, appreciate the complexity. Although our encounter was brief, I feel I now understand something of Javer's story and of how he ticks. To hear a one-time insurgent leader talk, to watch his eyes as he answers a difficult question, or to observe the pride with which he looks at his son on his bicycle, takes you a little closer to the man himself, and a little further from the easy cliché.

Jolo is trying hard to throw off its associations with the likes of ISIS and Abu Sayyaf and make the island as appealing as any in the Philippines. Its unofficial slogan, 'From Terrorism to Tourism', may be a little too honest, but there are some undoubted rewards for those who make the journey this far south. One such is the beachside restaurant-cum-coffee bar overlooking a wide bay dotted with rocky outcrops that we come across on our way back from Javer's house. Disco music blares out. When we arrive, the road outside is strewn with motorbikes and the tables out front are filling up fast, as this place has a growing reputation for good food and high-quality coffee. It's also clearly a social hub, as crowds of boys on bikes and girls in hijabs, also on bikes, keep coming all the time we're there. A hard-working young couple, Maya and her husband, opened the venue only recently. They have a strong commitment to the local community. She explains that the queues tonight are rather longer than usual because she is offering free meals for Ramadan.

As the sun goes down over the bay I feel a rush of elation. I'm exhausted. We're all exhausted. Travelling in a land of seven thousand

islands is a constant series of arrivals and departures, of packing and unpacking, of jumping out of small planes and into small boats. But we feel we have got to know the Philippines and that, after all, is the aim of these journeys. To go away having learnt something. To go away knowing the world a little better and a little more closely.

And there's a bit of unexpected good news as we line up for a last crew photo. After days and weeks of requests and refusals, we've learnt that the President will receive us on Saturday morning, our last day in the Philippines. He is, however, his people remind us, a very busy man and will only have time for three questions, which we must submit in advance.

The prospect of visiting a palace at the other end of the country after breakfast and flying home to the UK in the afternoon is a rather daunting one. The likelihood of it all coming off is down to the one unquantifiable factor in this last-minute saga. MV *Maria Rebecca*.

DAY 18

Back to Manila

THE GODS HAVE SMILED. WE MAY HAVE HAD TO PUT UP with another night on the hard bunks, but the sea was calm and there were no flying suitcases.

At Zamboanga unloading is brisk and we're soon at the airport for the flight back – or, in my case, the sleep back – to Manila.

Before too long we're in Adriatico Street once more and the comforting embrace of the Sheraton. Here we scratch our heads over the three questions we are allowed to put to the President tomorrow. It's clear that these will have to be pretty anodyne, so anything to do with China or terrorism or the name Duterte is out. Eventually we come up with: What do you love about the Philippines? How has the Philippines changed during your lifetime? What memories do you have of growing up in a presidential palace? Other, slightly more severe, candidates are rejected.

I enjoy a shower and a proper bed for the first time in three nights.

DAY 19

Manila

WE'RE UP AT SIX AND THEN GATHER IN THE LOBBY. We've all had to spruce ourselves up for the President, which has required the casting aside of the normal filming kit of T-shirts and jeans and the speedy purchase of dark trousers, dark shirts and, in my case, a new black jacket. No trainers are allowed, so we have all been decked out with black leather shoes. We look as though we're going to arrest somebody, not interview them.

It's early Saturday morning. The normally packed streets of Manila are weirdly empty as we make our way to the Malacañang, the official residence of the President. It's set in a gated area which includes shops and restaurants, with the palace itself – a handsome classical building – standing behind tall railings. After some time has

passed we're met by amiable security men and led through ornate cast-iron gates and up a path past a lawn lined with ancient trees to the entrance, where bags are searched and we're introduced to a number of minders, courtiers and PR people before being shown up a red-carpeted staircase to a floor full of immense rooms and side-chambers.

We're ushered into one of these side-rooms where a heavy oak table has been laid with breakfast and fresh coffee. The walls are adorned with an amazing collection of paintings by Grandma Moses, the great American folk artist who started painting at the age of seventy-eight. A less attractive piece of Americana sits in the back row of a celebrity photo table. It's a photo of Pete Hegseth, the Secretary for War, complete with tight jacket and matching smile. Sent with his best wishes.

Once we've had a sip of coffee and a bite of croissant we're led into a much more impressive room that somehow manages to project comfortable rather than overbearing power. Here, the walls are panelled with dark wood and decorated in Spanish style. Long white curtains and thick carpets create a muted effect. The wow factor is supplied by an enormous, elaborately carved wooden chandelier which hangs from a golden cupola in the ceiling.

The stage is set. Now we await the main player.

Delays are a common feature of interviews with people in power. They are often deliberately contrived to create a suspension of time and space – a sense of limbo that can only be given meaning by the arrival of someone more important than any of the rest of us.

After the requisite pause, there's a sudden buzz of animation. A series of quietly urgent messages alert us to the fact that the President is coming. The President of the Philippines is coming. I clear my throat, button my jacket and try to banish any feelings of intimidation.

A small man walks through a very lofty doorway. He wears a dark suit and big glasses and has a head of thick black hair. This is the man. Before I raise my hand, his is already out and a broad smile lights up his face. 'Michael Palin!' he declares. 'So good to meet you.' Suddenly the roles are reversed. He's the lucky one. I, apparently, am the VIP. He may be the president of the seventh-most populous country in Asia, but I am one of the *Monty Python* team. And he is a huge fan.

The son of Ferdinand and Imelda Marcos was, it turns out, educated in Britain, at a public school in Sussex and then at Oxford University. This was back in the early seventies when *Python* was building up quite a fanatical following, especially among students, and the future President was one of those who packed his college's common room to watch the latest episode on late-night TV. My carefully prepared three questions fly out of my head, and I find myself apologising for the fact that not everyone approved of *Python*'s jokes.

'That was part of the charm, wasn't it? The serious people didn't like it.'

His enthusiasm never wanes. He is keen to know how we came up with something like the Fish-Slapping Dance, and listens to my reply with rapt attention.

At one point, with a confidential nod, he motions me towards a room off the main hall.

'Come and have a look,' he beckons. 'This is my office. This is where I sign the various —' He breaks off. Despite much rattling of the handle the door won't budge. He tries again without luck. *Python* seems to have come to the palace.

'Oh dear,' he says despairingly, 'they won't even let me in my own office.'

But he's not discouraged and continues with his personal tour of the palace, in the process of which a three-question encounter turns into a forty-five-minute interview.

On the walls in the main chamber are some fine portraits of former presidents, including one of his father and one of his arch-rival

Rodrigo Duterte. He draws my attention to a painting of a thin-faced, swarthy man. 'That's our first president, Aguinaldo.'

Emilio Aguinaldo was the Simón Bolívar of the Philippines. He led a revolution against Spain in the last years of the nineteenth century, and declared the country a republic in 1898. But it didn't last. The Americans moved in to fill the vacuum left by the Spanish and captured Aguinaldo two years later. His dream of an independent Republic of the Philippines was not realised for another forty-six years.

The President points out the most famous painting in the collection. It's of Ferdinand Magellan bargaining with tribal leaders. 'Didn't they kill him?' I ask. 'Wasn't he killed by a local chieftain?' Bongbong nods, but assures me that he's still seen as a very important part of their history.

'We have places called Magallanes all over the Philippines.'

The President and his family live in a residence in Malacañang Park, on the other side of the Pasig river, and these grand rooms are now used only on ceremonial occasions. But this is where he was brought up. He recalls the strangeness of living amid all this opulence, of coming out of his room in pyjamas only to encounter his father walking past with some fellow world leader.

'Oh, this is my son,' he would announce. Bongbong remembers feeling embarrassed. 'I didn't have a dressing gown on, you know. Lessons of power,' he reflects. 'We were just kids trying to be normal.'

For some reason his use of the word 'normal' brings to mind his mother, Imelda – she of three thousand pairs of shoes – probably one of the least normal people in modern politics. She is now ninety-six, but, apparently, still going strong.

'I mean, we keep telling her to sit down and put down her memoirs.' But, he adds with a sigh, 'She's not the sort of person to sit down.'

We've been strolling around for half an hour before I finally get to ask one of the much-agonised-over three questions. How has the Philippines changed in his lifetime? He doesn't have to stop and think.

The population has more than tripled: from 35 million when he was a boy to 115 million now. The country has become more cosmopolitan. The diaspora has grown and more than ever are leaving to find work abroad. Bongbong recalls that when he first came to

England and walked down Kensington High Street he was the only Filipino around. Last time he was there he heard three Filipino dialects on the same street.

I ask him where the best Philippine food can be found in London.

'Well, if I'm in London and you're there, I'll come and cook for you.' My mind reels.

He feels optimistic about what's happening in the Philippines now. This year they hold the chair of ASEAN, the Association of South East Asian Nations.

'We're pulling the whole of South East Asia together.'

I don't like to ask about the power of the Chinese, whose trade surplus with the ASEAN nations rose by 45 per cent last year to $276 billion.

Finally Bongbong reflects on the Philippines' wider place in the world. Once they were very much in the American sphere of influence. Now, he says, they no longer feel they have to choose one side or the other. 'We are the Philippines. We do what's best for ourselves.'

On this upbeat note our improbably rich and laid-back conversation ends. It's been hell for Jaimie and his camera, and Joe with his mike, to keep up with us, but we're all grateful for how relaxed and revealing the President has made an encounter we had been led to believe would be short and formal.

We have photos taken together. When we emerge at last through the big black gates it's almost time to leave for the airport. We snatch a quick group photo.

It's a long flight home. By the evening we've only got as far as

Hong Kong. As the Chinese immigration officers bark orders at us, I find myself missing Philippine charm.

Fortunately the Middle East conflict, which blew up almost as soon as we got here, has not affected our flight. But it still takes over fourteen hours to pick our way south of Russia and north of Iran.

And that's a lot of movies.

POSTSCRIPT

PERHAPS IT'S MY AGE, OR PERHAPS IT'S JUST THAT IT'S further away, but I took longer to recover from our Philippine adventure than any of the others we've filmed and recorded.

I think it boils down to the archipelago effect. Just when you think you're somewhere there's another island beckoning across the water. And there are many more hotels, resorts and guest houses to tempt the traveller than I remember from my first visit, thirty years ago. In nineteen days we stayed at twelve different places.

All of which made for a feeling of restlessness, of always being on the move.

I felt that about the country, too. The Philippines is a scattering, both geographically and historically. It was getting on fine until the Spanish decided they wanted to live there as well. That somehow worked out until Emilio Aguinaldo tried to throw off the colonial shackles and lead the Philippines to independence, at which point the Americans decided they wanted to live there, too.

It's scarcely surprising that national unity in a country that has had such a complicated history should be something of a fragile flower. There's tension between the predominantly Roman Catholic north and the Muslim south. There's competition between the various islands that make up the archipelago and between the big cities: Manila, Cebu and Davao. And there's an extraordinary range of languages spoken: Filipino (the national language, based on Tagalog), English and more than a hundred others – some, like Kapampangan, Ilokano and Pangasinese, reflecting the country's Malaysian inheritance. Neighbours such as Japan and China are like strongboxes, fiercely protective of their status, history and way of life. The Philippines is more like an overstocked suitcase, with bits falling out here and there.

Which is what makes it both appealing and vulnerable.

As we flew out of Manila I heaved a sigh of relief. At last I could get some rest. But at the same time I felt real regret. After all, I wouldn't have needed the rest if I hadn't spent three weeks in such a rich, revealing, open-hearted country. We had seen, and been allowed to see, the underbelly of a country, but also its great beauty and encouraging signs of an awareness of the need for nature parks and biospheres to protect the prolific wildlife from predators. We'd snatched an impression of a nation trying to find its place in a fractured world. It is in all our interests to make sure its voice is heard over the roars of the big beasts.

CHRONOLOGY

*c.*55,000 BCE	First *Homo sapiens* in the Philippines
*c.*4000	Rice being cultivated
982 CE	Chinese record visit by traders from Philippines
*c.*1000	Buddhism and Hinduism established
1380	First mosque built, on Simunul Island
1521	Ferdinand Magellan reaches Philippines, and dies at battle of Mactan
1543	Ruy López de Villalobos arrives in Philippines
1579	Domingo de Salazar becomes first Bishop of Manila
1681–3	Zambal Revolt, one of many during the years of Spanish rule
1896	Emilio Aguinaldo leads Philippine Revolution against Spanish rule
1898	In the course of the Spanish-American War, US forces take Manila

1941 After their attack on Pearl Harbor, Japanese invade Philippines

1946 Treaty of Manila recognises independence of Philippines from US

1965 Ferdinand Marcos elected president of the Republic of the Philippines

1972 Marcos declares martial law

1986 Marcos overthrown and flees the country; Corazon Aquino becomes president

2016 Rodrigo Duterte becomes president

2017 Battle of Marawi

2022 Duterte defeated in presidential election by Ferdinand 'Bongbong' Marcos

2025 Duterte arrested at Ninoy Aquino International Airport and extradited to The Hague

MUSGIRLS
MIA

ACKNOWLEDGEMENTS

I HAVE MANY PEOPLE TO THANK FOR GETTING ME THERE and back.

My director, Neil Ferguson, was, once more, the heart and soul of the operation, visiting and researching the country in advance. Girlie Linao's experience and calm kept us all going, helped as she was by Maricris Calilung-McGuinness and Inky Nakpil.

My indefatigable crew were Jaimie Gramston DOP, with Alex Lobsang on second camera, Joe Morsman on sound, and Ryan Shelley as our medic and security officer.

I hugely appreciate the encouragement of Ian Rumsey and our executive producer, Jeremy Daldrey, at ITN, and the help and great support of Guy Davies at Five.

My own support team – Steve Abbott, Paul Bird and Mimi Robinson – were as indispensable as ever.

Nigel Wilcockson, my publisher, and his team have been towers of strength in bringing this book together.

Thank you all.

PHOTOGRAPHY

Photographs are reproduced by kind permission of:

Neil Ferguson pp. 19, 24, 26, 29, 32, 38, 43, 58, 75, 79, 85, 86, 97, 99, 100, 106, 113, 114, 115, 116 (top right), 117 (bottom right), 134, 150, 153, 155, 167.
Jaimie Gramston pp. viii, 10, 11, 12, 18, 31, 66, 72, 92, 93, 96, 98, 107, 130, 131, 132, 161, 162, 164, 176, 180.
Joe Morsman pp. 6, 13, 14, 16, 23, 27, 36, 40, 41, 44–45 46, 47, 49, 50–51, 52, 53, 55, 56, 60 (bottom), 64–65, 67, 73, 78, 88, 90, 94, 95, 102, 108, 116 (top left, top left middle, top right middle, middle left, middle, middle right, bottom left, bottom right), 117 (top left, bottom left), 118, 122, 124, 127, 128 (top), 133, 138, 140, 141, 142–143 (top), 142 (bottom), 143 (bottom), 144, 149, 150, 156, 168–169.
ITN Productions pp. 80, 105.

Getty p. 62 (TED ALJIBE).
Wikimedia Commons (https://creativecommons.org/licenses)
p. 8 (Patrickroque01, CC BY-SA 4.0),
p. 34 (Patrick Roque, CC BY-SA 4.0),
p. 54 (Jordan Balintac, CC BY-SA 4.0),
p. 89 (Øyvind Holmstad, CC BY-SA 4.0),
p. 110 (Patrickroque01, CC BY-SA 4.0),
pp. 146–147 (Patrickroque01, CC BY-SA 4.0),
p. 160 (Ramon FVelasquez, CC BY-SA 3.0).

All other photographs: **Michael Palin**

HUTCHINSON HEINEMANN

UK | USA | Canada | Ireland | Australia
India | New Zealand | South Africa

Hutchinson Heinemann is part of the Penguin Random House group of companies whose addresses can be found at global.penguinrandomhouse.com

Penguin Random House UK,
One Embassy Gardens, 8 Viaduct Gardens,
London SW11 7BW

penguin.co.uk

Penguin Random House UK

First published 2026
001

Publisher: Nigel Wilcockson

Assistant Editor: Hannah White-Steele

Copy-editor: Mary Chamberlain

Proofreader: Caroline Pretty

Designer: Tim Barnes
www.herechickychicky.com

Map: Darren Bennett
www.dkbcreative.com

Set in Chimanga 9pt

Printed and bound in Italy by L.E.G.O. S.p.A.

The authorised representative in the EEA is Penguin Random House Ireland, Morrison Chambers, 32 Nassau Street, Dublin D02 YH68

A CIP catalogue record for this book is available from the British Library

ISBN: 978-1-529-99592-3

Penguin Random House is committed to a sustainable future for our business, our readers and our planet. This book is made from Forest Stewardship Council® certified paper.

FSC
www.fsc.org
MIX
Paper
FSC® C018179